Awakening the Spirit Within

Yolanda Tarantino

Yolanda Tarantino

Disclaimer
This book contains the ideas and opinions of its author. The intention of this book is to provide information, helpful content, and motivation to readers about the subjects addressed. It is published and sold with the understanding that the author is not engaged to render any type of psychological, medical, legal, or any other kind of personal or professional advice. No warranties or guarantees are expressed or implied by the author's choice to include any of the content in this volume. The author shall not be liable for any physical, psychological, emotional, financial, or commercial damages, including, but not limited to, special, incidental, consequential, or other damages. The reader is responsible for their own choices, actions, and results.

1st Edition. 1st printing 2025
Cover Concept and Interior Design: Stephen Walters, Oxygen Publishing Inc.
Editor: Richard Tardif

Independently Published by
Oxygen Publishing Inc.
Montreal, QC, Canada
www.oxygenpublishing.com
ISBN: 978-1-998686-04-9
Imprint: Independently published

Dedication

This book is dedicated to all the people who have helped shape my life, in particular

Lynn and René Boucher,
Reverend Gilles Morin,
and my mother.

I would have never made it this far without remembering all the beautiful teachers, healers, friends and loved ones who have crossed my path and have been a part of my journey. I thank you all for the beautiful work you do on this Earth plane.

Yolanda Tarantino

Acknowledgment

This book would not have been possible without the collaboration of **Teresa Roti** who helped me during this journey.

Our lives unknowingly crossed paths many times. We worked at the same reception hall and and coincidently she went to school and was friends with my brother. I didn't know her at the time but our lives would intersect later in life, when it was meant to be and for a more significant purpose.

Yolanda Tarantino

Contents

Yolanda Tarantino

Introduction

My intention for this book is to awaken the spirit within you. What I share comes from my own lived experiences and what I've learned through them. I'm a Reverend at the Spiritual Healing Church in Montreal, where I teach spiritual classes. I am a Reiki master and a shaman. I've dedicated my life to helping people heal from within: mind, body, and soul.

Through the gifts of the Holy Spirit of Truth, I receive visions from the spiritual realm. I speak with angelic beings and helpers, serving as a bridge between this world and the unseen world. My path has led me to live in service to God, and my mission is simple: to share what I've accepted in the hopes of empowering YOU to heal.

Even in the most painful moments, you are not meant to remain a victim. You were born to rise from the ashes.

Jesus Christ is my mentor. I can see His face and feel His presence. Within His consciousness and love I've found the strength to continue, again and again. I want to help you uncover that same strength, that untapped potential that lives within you, waiting to be awakened.

My journey has not been easy. I have been broken—more than once. I've wandered far from my true calling. But underneath all of it, my desire was always the same: I wanted to be whole. I longed to understand every part of myself: light and dark, broken and beautiful. I tried to speak with angels and with those who had passed from this world. I wanted to hear God's voice and learn how to live in His grace.

Awakening the Spirit Within comes from that longing and from what I've learned in my pursuit of divine connection. My life is now dedicated to soul-to-soul connection: to witnessing the sacred unfold in others, and to walking beside them as they begin their healing journey with God.

Life is a lot like childbirth. There's pain, struggle, even anguish—but when the suffering passes, something new is born. You begin to see life differently. You understand, deeply, that you are part of something greater: a collective consciousness, a divine circle of life.

We are all here to learn, to evolve, and to grow closer to the truth. I believe that God wants us to know, beyond all doubt, that no matter how much we suffer, we are unconditionally loved. And yet, being disconnected from God leaves us in the dark. Trauma, grief, rejection, especially when they come early in life, can be doorways for dark forces to sneak in. This separation can begin as early as the womb.

Anything that fragments the connection between our mind, body, and soul leads us further into darkness. And when thoughts come: God doesn't love me, or I'm not worthy of His love, we need to stop and ask ourselves: Where is this coming from?

Let me be clear: those are not your thoughts. They are outside influences, forces that seek to pull you away from God. The Bible speaks of these as principalities and powers, real spiritual forces that wage war in the unseen realms. Part of the purpose of this book is to open your eyes to this truth.

I believe there is evil in the world, and its mission is to keep us away from the light of God. There are malevolent spirits that feed on human suffering. Their goal is to keep you in torment so your soul never finds peace. Here is Satan's plan—to lure you away from your divine purpose by offering you something false. Instead of praising the Lord, we begin to worship the idols of this world: power, money, and self-obsession. These distractions are designed to make us forget who we are in God.

Anything that causes you to doubt God's presence, His power, or His love is not from God.

"We are one body in union with Christ."
Romans 12:5

Jesus taught us this openly. A real relationship with God isn't just spiritual—it's supernatural. It's nothing to fear, and certainly nothing to be ashamed of.

It is something to embrace.

We are souls living in physical bodies. There is a difference between the soul and the spirit:

- The **soul** is where we feel, think, and will. It holds our emotions, our desires, and our ego.
- The **spirit** comes from God: the Infinite, the Omnipotent, the Source of all life.

When our spirit is renewed, we begin to walk in unity with God. But to truly be whole, we must care for more than just the physical. We must also recognize our emotional, mental, and spiritual aspects. Through prayer, meditation, and inner work, we can align them and begin the process of healing.

It begins with the heart: choosing to forgive and choosing to release anger, jealousy, or resentment, and choosing love. Without these choices we remain trapped in cycles of pain.

My most profound hope is that through the pages of this book you will begin your healing journey—one that leads you into wholeness, and ultimately, into union with Christ.

Let your healing begin.

Yolanda Tarantino

Chapter 1

Humble Beginnings

To understand where I come from and why I walk the path I do, I have to start with my roots.

My father, Angelo Tarantino, came from Avelino, a small village near Naples, Italy. Around 1956 at the age of 16, he left home to work in Germany, as many young men did at the time. Eleven years later in 1967, at the age of 27, he immigrated to Canada in search of a better life. His sister, my Aunt Yolanda, was already settled in Canada and sponsored him, along with four other siblings. My mother, Estelle Guimond, was Métis, of mixed European and Indigenous heritage, with French, Mohawk, and Mi'kmaq bloodlines.

My maternal great-grandmother, Rose Ludivine Mazerolle, was of full Mi'kmaq descent but had been adopted by a French family in the late 1800s. Native blood runs in my veins, tracing back at least three generations. My grandfather's wife, Melina, was also Métis. She was deeply spiritual, having been raised Catholic, and prayed the Holy Rosary, attending church regularly.

Melina was a woman of great faith. My mom remembers how my grandmother would ask her children to kneel and pray the rosary with her every night. She was a small woman, standing at four foot, ten inches and weighing between 90 and 100 pounds. She bore many children but also endured many failed pregnancies—my mother believes Melina may have been pregnant 24 times. Despite multiple miscarriages, she gave birth to seven daughters and two sons. Sadly, three of the nine children died from rare illnesses, and my mom's brother, Alex, was only 10 when he passed away from meningitis.

My grandmother had the gift of healing. People in the village would go to her for skin conditions, such as warts, and she would take her wedding band,

---

make the sign of the cross on the affected area, and watch the warts disappear. She was also known for her gift of prophecy and practised tasseography, the art of divining and interpreting messages found in tea leaves.

Life was hard. My grandfather, Alex, was a fisherman in Miramichi Bay, New Brunswick, where my mother's family lived. With so many mouths to feed, they all relied on his catch to eat, sell, and buy other food. Sometimes, my grandmother would tell him, "You're going to have a good catch this week, Alex. I see many salmon!" As predicted he would return with a great bounty.

Her faith, love for God, music, and her role as a loving mother brought her the most joy. Tragically, on June 6th, 1956, at 41, three hours after giving birth to my Aunt Gladys, Melina passed away because of post-birth complications. My mother was 12.

Whenever a shift is near, whether good or troubling, I feel Melina's spirit draw close to reassure me.

Connections

While my bloodline carried Indigenous roots, it was through lived experience and spiritual practice that I came to understand their meaning. I've always felt such a deep connection to Indigenous culture, particularly First Nations music: the sound of their flutes, drumming, and dancing. So, in 2017, I bought a drum and attended my first powwow, an Algonquian healing rite: a sacred gathering where Indigenous peoples sing, dance, and honour ancestral traditions.

I began drumming at home, listening to different vocal sounds. Guided by my love of music, I taught myself to drum to the beat. It came naturally to me.

However, the beautiful simplicity of Indigenous traditions in embracing the Spirit always connected with the Great Spirit, captivated me most. There's no barrier between the Creator and creation; God is in all things. Indigenous people pray and offer blessings in everything they do. When they hunt, they do not kill for sport but take only what is necessary for survival, giving thanks, and using every part without waste. I was moved by how they respect Mother Earth; their reverence reminded me of my grandmother's healing ways.

In Indigenous traditions, spiritual warfare is met head-on in a distinctly different manner. Medicine people, also known as shamans, are trained to sense and address the presence of evil. Their skills and wisdom are passed down through generations, forming a sacred lineage of healing and protection.

In 2011, I was fortunate to meet a First Nations chief. I was attending a metaphysical convention where I was giving spiritual readings. He was in a booth selling handmade crafts, books, and CDs. I told him that I had Native Indian blood and purchased a CD. I returned to my booth as I had a spiritual reading to give. After I had finished my reading he approached me and we started a conversation.

While chatting, I received a message and shared it with him. In the vision, I saw two wise and old figures watching. I described them, and he explained they had been his elders and teachers, and that no one had ever described them in such vivid detail. Later that day he presented me with a gift. A feather! He explained this was a rare feather from an eagle. Emotion welled up before I could speak.

Later, I learned that receiving an eagle feather from a chief is one of the highest honours in Indigenous culture—something rarely given and never lightly. When he placed it in my hands, I felt an overwhelming sense of recognition, as if I'd seen something ancient within. I still have that feather. It holds a sacred place in my life, symbolizing Spirit, guidance, and deep belonging. I remember who I am and the path I walk. I use it for ceremonial purposes, such as traditional smudging with white sage to remove negative energy from my home and body.

Belonging

As much as I felt connected to my native roots and despite coming from diverse racial and cultural backgrounds, I always tried to understand where I truly belonged. Discovering my great-grandmother's background helped me understand my close connection, admiration, and respect for Indigenous traditions and spiritual practices. I relate to their belief in the Great Spirit. I love their music—it moves me. It is the Spirit in motion and energy. My search for God has led me down this path.

God wants me to share these experiences with you. He is gathering all of humanity to him. If you are searching as I once was, and you have this void inside that wants more, search your heart for the truth. Ask God to intercede for you through His son, Jesus Christ. When you invoke the Spirit in union through the heart and mind of Christ, God begins to reveal Himself.

> *"The Lord God formed the man from the dust of the ground and breathed into his nostrils the breath of life, and the man became a living being."*

(Genesis 2:7)

Chapter 2

Early Childhood

In 1969, my mother worked as a waitress at an A&W in LaSalle, Quebec. In those days where A&W had drive-ins, servers would head out to parked cars to take orders and then return with their food. My father stood out from the crowd with his nice black Chevrolet Camaro. When my mother went to take his order, they started flirting.

Within two or three dates she was pregnant with me.

My mother already had two children out of wedlock with two other men. She gave birth to her first child at 19 and gave him up for adoption. However, she kept her second child and my older sister, Melina.

This time, she was 26 and pregnant with me. Since my father was not in the picture, my mother's sister suggested she give me up for adoption as well. My mother also thought this might be the best for everyone.

A child is a soul from its conception in the womb. It feels a mother's joys and pains and everything in between. My soul felt this rejection and abandonment from the very beginning. My life's journey revolved around a cycle of violence, instability, and abuse. Today, I realize that these challenges were ones I faced early in life, which helped me overcome various hardships and develop self-acceptance. You can't look outside yourself to feel whole—being whole comes from loving yourself.

But things changed once my mother gave birth to me. When she saw my precious face, she became consumed with love and decided to keep me. She named me Yolanda, which coincidentally was not only a popular name at the time, but also the name of my father's older sister. She would later play a significant part in my life.

We were poor and lived on the second floor of a two-bedroom apartment in LaSalle. My older sister was four at that time. There was no crib, so my mother made a bed out of a dresser drawer by stapling some cushions around the inside. That's where I slept for the first three months of my life.

Her brother, Gary, was a musician and lived with us. He played music for me while I was sitting in my high chair. Apparently, my eyes would light up when he played. He played a lot of country music and I loved listening to him. He ignited my love of music. Music would become my solace in life.

My father was in Italy visiting his sister, Yolanda. She found a picture of me in his pants pocket while doing laundry. After some probing he admitted he'd had a child out of wedlock. His family encouraged him to do the right thing, return to Canada and marry my mother. Maybe it would have been better had he not returned, but then I would not have learned the lessons for my soul's advancement.

My first memory of my father dates back to when I was four years old. He returned home from one of his gambling escapades in a rage. He smashed one of my mother's high heels over her head. Her screams still ring in my ears. Children are innocent until someone breaks that innocence and destroys their trust. When trust is lost they grow into adults who distrust everyone.

A Life Of Trauma

From 1974 to 1980, violence, trauma, chaos, turmoil, and instability plagued my life. I continued to witness a string of physical abuse at home between my father and my mother.. In 1975, I watched him smash my mother's head on the table. Why? She didn't have his food prepared and on the table by the time he got home from hunting.

My living circumstances also interfered with my capacity to focus on school, and I had to repeat the fourth grade. We moved again in 1980, this time to a house we had purchased on Rue de Lanaudière in the Villeray district of Montreal, and completely gutted the basement. When my aunt from New Brunswick visited, she was horrified by our living conditions. Our basement was rat infested, and she begged my mother to return to New Brunswick, knowing that my father was quite abusive. My mother reluctantly agreed and packed up some of our belongings, and we secretly escaped during the night while my father was at work. She left him a long letter.

My father was so angry that he came after us. It was March and my father used the excuse that he was going hunting, and we were his prey. He got into a car accident and my uncle had to pick him up somewhere along the highway between Rivière-du-Loup and Fredericton. My father had packed hunting rifles, and when he arrived he threatened my mother that he would kill her, my sister, my brother, and me if we didn't return. Out of fear for our lives, my mother agreed.

I was so devastated and angry at my mother for agreeing to go back. I was just getting readjusted in a new school where I felt safe and was doing well. I resented her, not fully understanding her fear of my father. We returned home, and the cycle of abuse and violence continued. Nothing changed.

During the summer of 1981, I was 11, and I witnessed my mother get brutally beaten again by my father. It was my mother's 38th birthday, and two good neighbours (my mother's friends) invited her to celebrate. My mother was often alone and didn't go out, and my father was working at the reception hall, and her friends didn't want her to be alone on her birthday.

When my father came home at midnight and saw that my mother wasn't home, he became furious. He entered my bedroom, sat in the chair holding a wooden broomstick, and threatened that if I tried to stop him from confronting her when my mother walked through the door, I would receive the brunt of his anger. I was protective of my mother, so when I heard her coming down the street and saying good night to her friends, I screamed through the window for her not to enter the house. I tried to warn her many times not to come in, but he told me to sit down and keep quiet.

Unfortunately, she didn't hear my warnings.

When she walked in, he unleashed a horrific and brutal monster. What transpired was pure evil. I witnessed absolute cruelty. I believe that a demon had taken hold of my father and fed off his negative thoughts and emotions. How my mother survived that beating is only thanks to the Grace of God. The number of hits she took to her head and lashes to her back seemed endless. I couldn't do anything to stop it.

Yolanda Tarantino

Chapter 3

Helpless

My mother's bruises told a story that no one should live through. I couldn't speak. I froze. My mother's screams alerted our neighbour, Armand, who came running. He punched my father and pulled him off my mother. I could not fathom what would have happened had Armand not intervened. I believe the supernatural stepped in. I am forever grateful to him.

My mother pressed charges and placed a restraining order against him. We also had Ville Marie Services of Greater Montreal assign a few social workers to us. My mother didn't feel safe staying in the house, so we spent six weeks that summer at my Uncle Gary's in Lachine.

False Hope

My mother brought us home again when I started Grade Six. The social workers tried to help, but my mother insisted on having her way. So they kept a close eye on us.

Over the Christmas holidays, I discovered that my mother was sneaking out to meet my father. She felt sorry for him and said she wanted to take him back. My mom loved my dad to the core of her soul. How much did one person have to endure? I could not understand this. But he was a skilled manipulator who knew how to exploit her vulnerabilities to keep the family together.

In January 1982, my father moved back in with us.

Not long after, a social worker strongly recommended removing me and my siblings from home and school after another violent altercation between our parents. We uprooted again, this time to a battered women's shelter, where we stayed for three and a half months. I went to another new school, Saint Monica's. During this period, my aunt and uncle from New Brunswick had moved to Ottawa. So we moved again!

Aunt Patricia welcomed us once more. I enrolled at Belair School to finish Grade Six. I enjoyed being in a new city where no one knew me. More of my mother's family surrounded us: Aunt Monica, who had three daughters, and Aunt Anne-Marie, who had two daughters. I spent most of my time with my cousin, Brenda, who was a year older than I, and Jenny, who was one year younger. I felt safe for the first time and began to excel in school.

Cycles of Escape

But Melina, my sister, hated being in Ottawa and didn't feel like she belonged. She was 17 years old and missed her old life in Montreal. She returned to Montreal to be with her friends, leaving my brother and me behind. I thought her actions were selfish, but she was just as much a victim. I was so wrapped up in myself that I never asked about her pain. She was doing what she needed to survive.

While we were in Ottawa my father came for a surprise visit. I should've seen it coming. My mother had applied for social housing, but the next thing I knew she had packed us up and moved back to Montreal. We had no choice. My mother never asked how moving again might affect us. Leaving Ottawa felt like another betrayal. I didn't know how to trust the ground beneath me.

So, we returned to Montreal and settled in LaSalle. I enrolled at LaSalle Catholic Comprehensive High School (LCCHS) to begin Grade Seven. It was yet another fresh start.

I began the new year with a new attitude. I didn't have to deal with any bullying, but when things got too stressful or I faced a challenge, I would retreat inward and hide. I also experienced social awkwardness. I was often embarrassed because I had to see the school priest at lunch to get a food voucher for the cafeteria. People didn't know who I was or what I was going through at home. I wouldn't do my homework and kept to myself. My teachers suspected something was wrong, but they didn't know what.

Luckily, I became friends with Father Shaw, the priest assigned to the school. I often visited him during the classes I avoided: Math and History. I loved French, Religion, Arts, Music, and English. He became my teacher and saving grace during my three years at LCCHS. He was like a father figure to me. Every day, I asked him searching questions about life. He was a superb listener and understood my difficulties.

He oversaw my first chance to perform. We met in the chapel to rehearse for the school variety show, where I found solace in singing. Singing made me feel safe, helped me heal, and gave me the confidence I needed. I would get chills and feel the Spirit of God within me.

I stayed at LCCHS until I turned 15. By the time I reached Grade 10, I switched to another school because of my new friend and neighbour, Tammy. I spent a lot of time with Tammy, and I thought it would be beneficial to attend the same school as her. But it turned out to be a disaster. After six months I became depressed, and went back and forth between my mother's house and the pocket of calm that was Aunt Yolanda's house.

At the same time Melina was acting out and my mother just focused on keeping the family together, but at what cost?

Lost in Darkness

There were still many dark years ahead for me, but all the trauma I was experiencing was to prepare me for my true calling—helping others heal through the Word of God.

But why was my trauma so crucial in my calling? How can I relate if I haven't known that kind of pain or have not shed those same tears? I would eventually come to understand why.

During one visit with Father Shaw, I discussed astrology and told him I had started reading the horoscope pages in the newspapers. He looked at me and said firmly, "Promise me you will never delve into the occult experiences." He never explained why, and I didn't ask. I enjoyed astrology. I would read the horoscopes and sneak off to psychic fairs with friends behind my parents' backs.

That was when I began slipping into the occult life.

When I was 16, my friend Elisa and I would play with tarot cards and ask the cards questions. We didn't take it seriously. I tested the limits of the supernatural using a Ouija board, a game that allows communication with spirits.

One Friday night, while my mother was at Bingo and my father was out drinking, I invited friends to play with my homemade Ouija board. I lit a candle and then we put our hands on the glass. As it moved around the board, it spelled out my name and said I was evil. I was petrified, and everyone was in a state of shock. Suddenly, my white blouse caught on fire from the candle and burned my left shoulder—I still have the scar. My mother walked in on us and everyone scattered. She began praying with her crucifix in the name of our Lord Jesus that the evil spirit present be gone from our house.

Although I didn't conjure a true spirit, I didn't know that when you play in uncharted territory, you can open lower levels of the astral plane, which allows a gateway for wicked, malevolent spirits to pass through. These harmful spirits lie in wait for foolish, innocent children who are playing with fire—literally. We didn't realize that we could open energy vortexes, allowing these spirits to attach themselves to our energy. They wreaked havoc by tormenting us without our knowledge.

I continued on my path of destruction. I drank, acted out, and strayed far from God's calling.

Chapter 4

Breaking Patterns

In 1989, I turned 18 and our family moved into a lovely three-bedroom apartment in LaSalle. I was working at a pharmacy and having a great time. I started to explore my sexuality and became promiscuous. During this time, my brother Angelo started high school, and my sister Melina, who my mother had kicked out of the house two years earlier on her birthday, followed in our mother's footsteps by becoming pregnant and having her first child out of wedlock at the age of 20.

At 19, I was accepted into Dawson College and attended night school as a mature student. But I did not feel I could function. I was fighting through so many traumatic experiences and dark moments, and needed to push through to see the light.

Right after the holidays, I was on the verge of a mental breakdown. My parents' marriage was still horrible. My father was gambling heavily, cheating on my mother, and frequently going to bars. One night he came home in one of his fits of rage. My mother had made pasta with sauce. He grabbed the plate and smashed it on the floor. Spaghetti and sauce flew everywhere.

I threw my plate and cup at him yelling, "How does it feel to have something thrown at you? Don't you dare touch her!"

He lunged at me, grabbed my hair and punched me in the head. I threatened him, saying I was going to call the police and they were going to throw him back in jail. As soon as I picked up the phone he backed off. With a prior conviction, it would not bode well for him if he got arrested again.

After that, my mother decided to go on a silent retreat in Lancaster, Ontario, at the encouragement of Father Shaw. She left me alone and responsible for my 12-year-old brother. Angelo was so upset on that first day that he ran away from school in the afternoon, but thankfully returned home later the same day.

While my mother was away, I invited a friend to my house one day. She had always felt comfortable at my place and was already there when I arrived from college. While she waited, my father made sexual advances on her. When I got home, she confided in me. I was devastated. Angelo witnessed the entire ordeal.

It was no surprise that my father denied everything. There was no reason why my friend would make up such a thing; what that poor girl had to endure.

I was so angry I fell into an even darker place.

My brother had had enough and told my mother, while she was at the retreat, that she had to make a choice. If she wanted to be with her husband, then she would lose her son.

My mother reflected on what my brother had told her, and according to her, she experienced a series of supernatural occurrences. She spent three days in silence and started having night terrors, where a demon on a motorcycle was chasing her and my father. On the third day, she dreamt my father was going to hit her and told me about it. In the dream, he said, "Who's going to stop me from hitting you?"

Suddenly, a strong wind like a hurricane rose before my father, and a voice said, "I WILL."

My father asked, "Who are you?"

And the wind replied, "I am that I am," and took my father away.

My mother had clarity for the first time in her life and knew she would be okay. She returned home, packed up everything and left my father for the last time, breaking the pattern of abuse that had plagued her for the majority of her adult years.

It was a challenging time for all of us. We had little to no money for food. We visited food banks until we were able to receive welfare. I started working to help out. Although we barely had any money, my mother would buy my brother his expensive cold cuts because that's what he wanted. It annoyed me.

At 19, like my sister, I continued in my mother's footsteps and got pregnant. I met Drew at a club in downtown Montreal. After dating, we would go to his house and have sex. I was so naïve and let him convince me the pullout method was safe. I spent most of my time at his place during Christmas that year. We broke up shortly after. The following February I learned I was pregnant. I wasn't ready to be a mother. I didn't tell Drew.

I will never forget the day I scheduled an appointment to terminate my pregnancy. It was March 16th, 1989. My family had been living in a slightly rundown apartment building on Bayne in LaSalle. My sister came to pick me up after the procedure. I was a mess, mentally and emotionally. I felt an immense amount of guilt and was a lost soul. When we returned home, I locked myself in my room and cried for days.

After three days of tears, I picked up a Bible and asked God again and again to forgive me. I began to find my way back to Him. I laid it all down. Everything I'd been holding inside, I offered up. From that moment, the guilt lifted. I felt clean. Whole. The weight was gone. It was my turn to stop the cycle. I had a new sense of purpose—why was I here? What was I made for?

Yolanda Tarantino

Chapter 5

Turning My Life Around

Having an abortion forced me to turn my life around.

I became celibate, stopped drinking, and began helping my mother. I felt like I had control. I started attending night school and in December 1990, I met Steve, a man who would change my life. He would become my husband, partner, and soulmate in my search for truth.

We met in an adult education school in Lachine. He was in the military as an engineer. I was 19, so I could join the military without requiring parental consent. So, I joined the reserves in his engineering regiment in Montreal.

Steve and I began as friends, often grabbing coffee at Dunkin' Donuts to chat. He was easy to talk to—and he truly listened. He saw me!

We spent most of the holidays together and became a couple in January 1991. We spent time getting to know one another and developed a strong connection. We didn't kiss for six months. Our relationship was slower, deeper, and built on a foundation of friendship and trust. We'd go for long walks and talks at Saint Helen near Montreal.

During one hike, we sat on a bench and just looked at each other. We belonged. We felt a spiritual connection as if we knew each other from a former life. More specifically, our former life during the Crusades. We believed we came back in this lifetime to finish what we started.

When Steve came for dinner with my family, he learned that my mother had given her first child up for adoption. He decided to ask my mother if she wanted to search for him. She agreed, and Steve found my brother.

Over time, my gifts, which I had been denying, grew stronger. Love filled my heart, pushing out the weight of all I had endured, making room to empathize with others.

I knew I needed to heal and become whole.

Healing awakened the spirit. Without it, pain blocks light, and nothing can grow in darkness. How can love enter when pain, hatred, and resentment already occupy your heart? How can you receive God's love or gifts without room for love?

Meeting Steve allowed love to fill my heart and opened me up to God's love. It enhanced the gifts I had long buried.

My third eye chakra also kicked into high gear. The third eye chakra, also known as the Ajna chakra, is the sixth chakra, said to be located between your eyebrows at the bridge of your nose, parallel to the middle of your eyebrows, and the opening to one's clairvoyance and intuition.

My relationship with Steve opened my heart and activated my third eye chakra allowing my real journey of spiritual discovery to begin.

Chapter 6

First Supernatural Experience

My first spiritual experience, a testament to the existence of the supernatural, happened in August 1975.

I had just turned five, and my family was at our country home in Sainte-Anne-des-Plaines, Quebec. I was there with my parents and Melina, Aunt Yolanda, her husband, and their two children, Maria (12) and Tony (8). At the time, my mother was pregnant with Angelo. We had just finished eating lunch and were all supposed to go swimming at the lake.

Aunt Yolanda didn't want Tony to go because he had been sick with the flu. My uncle told my aunt to just let him have some fun. In those days, Italian men tended to dominate most decisions, so we all went to the lake, except for my aunt and mother, who stayed behind at the house.

At some point while everyone was playing, I remember singing and being led away from the lake. At such a tender age, children can perceive or experience things that adults cannot. However, they can't always explain them. Somehow, I found my way back home. My mother and my aunt were talking about my mother's brother Alex, who had died of meningitis when he was 10 years old.

I approached both of them and said, "Little Tony is dead!"

Startled, my mother stood up and slapped me, shouting, "Don't say things like that!" The fear that gripped me in that moment was overwhelming. Even though I had spoken the truth, from that moment I suppressed everything I heard or felt. My mother slapped me for relaying the message, which, as I later understood, came from her deep-seated fear, ignorance and religious beliefs. Satan and evil work their way subtly into our lives this way. I was now afraid to speak the truth as that meant loved ones would reject me. This fear hindered my ability to recognize, understand, and accept my gifts.

My aunt was shocked and wondered why I would say that little Tony was dead. Meanwhile, my father had found Tony's lifeless body and called the police and ambulance. The paramedics tried to revive him. An hour later the local police pulled into the cottage driveway and broke the sad news.

The white wolf experience

The night before Tony's death, my pregnant mother woke up in the middle of the night feeling hot, so she went outside and sat in my father's car. She was admiring the full moon when she glanced at the gated entrance of the cottage and saw a white wolf approach.

The sight was disturbing and confusing because white wolves were not a common sight in the area. She screamed and ran back into the house. My uncle and father grabbed their rifles and ran outside to find the wolf but saw nothing.

After Tony's unfortunate death, she realized the wolf had been sent as a warning. She had forgotten about this experience until years later, when a priest told her she had received a spiritual warning. In Indigenous cultures, animals can be spirit guides. They appear to help guide or protect you during your journey on this earth. Generally speaking animals will share or embody specific characteristics with you and help you understand the world around you. They can also reveal whether you use your instincts and intuition to grasp a situation. Unfortunately, my mother did not recognize the wolf's meaning.

The series of childhood visitations

Not long after this incident I began having night terrors. One night, my sister and I were in bed, and when I was about to fall asleep a large brownish mass of energy appeared between my bed and the window. I could feel the rage vibrating from this energy. The fear that possessed me was debilitating. I screamed and woke her up. My sister saw it as well. We looked at each other in disbelief before hiding under the covers. As quickly as it appeared, the mass of energy disappeared. We wanted to tell our parents but we knew we couldn't. They would never believe us or be receptive enough to hear us out. I remember having horrific nightmares as a child. One time, I woke up and a woman was floating in my room, trying to chase me. Then she disappeared. I believe she aimed to scare me. Again, I hid under the covers, shivering with fear. I never told my parents about that experience either. Now I understand those visits were demonic energies. I believe their ultimate goal was to instill fear in me to keep me away from God, to keep me in the dark about who God truly is, and how God works in our lives by healing us from pain and suffering. The devil attacks those with spiritual gifts who are closest to God as they pose the most risk to his plan of domination.

Another incident occurred when we lived in a two-bedroom apartment in Montreal's Villeray neighbourhood. I slept in a double bed with my sister. We would go to sleep feeling terrified as if something was watching us. One night, I was looking at my dresser and saw a tall shadow staring at me. It looked like a demon. I let out a scream and it evaporated into thin air.

On another occasion, when we lived in a basement apartment in LaSalle, I offered up my bed to some visitors who came to stay with us. That night I slept on the couch. I remember my back was facing the wall, and as I drifted off to sleep I felt something touch the back of my neck. I turned around and saw a lime green ghoulish creature; it looked like a goblin and I froze. I mustered up the courage and turned on all the lights in the living room, but there was nothing there. I couldn't sleep for the rest of the night. I fought my exhaustion out of fear that the creature would reappear, but eventually I fell asleep with the lights on. I didn't understand I was already picking up on demonic energies or energies of people who had passed on—a scared little kid seeing what I thought were monsters and ghosts.

Does evil exist? I believe it does! I believe demonic spirits can attach themselves to us, especially if there's a tear in the protective auric field or if trauma enters our lives. I have also seen these evil spirits oppress many other people. These types of evil spirits can weigh you down and make normal life very challenging.

Spiritual understanding

It's not easy to go deep within and look at all the parts of ourselves to truly understand the areas of our lives that aren't working and why. It is essential to do so, because it's when the tiny voice inside of us can truly sing. That voice is intuition from the highest source; listening to the small voice when we're in stillness is how the spirit anoints us. It happens to everyone, even non-believers. We have all been angry with God. You get a new job, which is God's path, and then three months later you are let go. You didn't even have the time to warm up the desk chair! You question why this is happening and what you are supposed to do now!

Six months later, you may have an even better opportunity with higher pay, better benefits, etc. Or maybe the entire company goes bankrupt. The point is, everything in life happens for a reason. When something negative happens, we can't see any positives or how this situation could possibly benefit us. We only understand once something positive has happened later, or that we have grown and evolved from the 'negative' situation. What's important is to allow God to show us the path.

"All yet a time is coming and has now come when the true worshipers will worship the Father in spirit and Truth, for they are the kind of worshipers the Father seeks. God is Spirit, and his worshipers must worship in spirit and in truth."

(John 4:23-24)

Chapter 7

First Spiritual Vision

In July 1977, when I was seven years old, I suffered something no one should ever have to endure—I was sexually molested.

My mother and father had attended a wedding and left me to stay overnight with our neighbour across the street, who usually babysat me. During this visit, she enacted some horrible and inappropriate sexual acts on me, which marked me for life. I felt so ashamed as if I were the one at fault. I felt dirty, unclean, and I blocked it out as if it never happened. I carried guilt for years. It wasn't until my early twenties that I began to acknowledge what had really happened.

Opening up helped me realize how this experience had cost me the ability to have healthy relationships with women, especially my mother. I realized that keeping everything bottled up was what led to my anxiety and health issues. Abuse and violence between my parents left me scared and traumatized.

Then something amazing happened—I had my first spiritual visitation.

I was in the fourth grade and had to stay late for tutoring. Afterwards, I walked home alone feeling uneasy and constantly looking around me. I felt the urge to look up and witnessed this huge window open in the sky. It was breathtaking. A woman with ruby red lips appeared before me wearing a beautiful veil, holding a bouquet of red roses in her left hand and cradling baby Jesus on her lap with her right hand.

It was Mother Mary, and she was smiling at me. I thought I was losing my mind and imagining things. How could this be real? Being a logical child, I told myself this couldn't be happening. Maybe if I closed my eyes and opened them again, the vision would be gone. So I did, but she was still there, smiling down at me as if she knew what I was thinking. Hope and promise filled me, yet I still wasn't sure what I was experiencing.

Eventually, I understood her presence that day was to let me know she would always be there for me. She knew my suffering and wanted to tell me that I was not alone, that my life would be difficult, but God my Father, and she, Mother Mary, would be there for me no matter how bad things got.

Suffering would take place in my life to allow me to develop a sense of empathy and insight. How could I relate and help others if I didn't learn to forgive my abusers and aggressors? I had to be able to comfort and tell others that I knew what they were going through and how they felt.

After my vision of Mother Mary, I attended Sunday service. I confided in what I had experienced, seeking guidance from our parish priest, Father Crispi, of Our Lady of Consolata Church in Montreal. I sat in confession and told him everything. I wanted to understand what this vision meant, as I was only seven and didn't have the insight to comprehend it fully.

To my dismay, he abruptly shut me down and told me there was no way I could have possibly seen Mother Mary; she would never have appeared before me. He accused me of being a liar and an attention seeker. His comments made me question any gifts that I may have possessed. My loyalty to the Catholic religion turned sour. I felt rejected and lost.

I put the Catholic Church on the back burner and moved away from it. I kept my vision a secret for years and never told anyone, except Father Shaw. Thankfully, I had a place to escape. My sister would take me to church every Sunday morning so I could sing my heart out during mass. It was the only thing that brought me any joy and peace. Church and singing were the only places I felt God's presence and His joy in my life. I felt a connection and a closeness to God that I didn't feel anywhere else.

My teachers at school also took an interest in my singing, and I was involved in many school shows and concerts. My school was part of the English Montreal School Board, which comprised five schools associated with the Consolata Church. I remember it was during the time I was preparing for my Confirmation. (Confirmation is the third of seven sacraments, a rite of passage in the Catholic religion.)

Every Sunday during Lent, each school presented in front of the congregation. (Lent is the five weeks leading up to Easter Sunday in the Christian religion.) When our turn came, we sang "Hallelujah," and every time I got up to sing that song, I felt the spirit of the Lord upon me.

Chapter 8

Unexplainable Occurrences

After a few years of dating, Steve and I moved into an apartment in Verdun. His grandfather had gifted us two beautiful glass ashtrays; delicate pieces etched with antique cars, because Steve had been especially close to his grandfather, who was a smoker.

On May 12th, 1992, while washing one of those ashtrays, it suddenly cracked in half in my hands. At that very moment, I heard a voice in my head: *Steve is about to get a call. His grandfather is in a car accident.*

Seconds later, the phone rang. It was Steve's aunt. His grandfather had been rushed to the emergency room at Montreal General. The doctors had found lung cancer that had spread to his brain, which they believed caused the accident.

Months later, on September 6th, I was holding the second ashtray when I heard another sharp crack—it too broke clean in half! A chill ran through me because in that moment I knew his grandfather had just passed. Within half an hour, Steve's mother called to confirm it.

Years passed. On December 4th, 1996, Steve and I were sitting in the living room with another glass ashtray on the coffee table. I wasn't smoking; just watching when, without warning it shattered! The TV flicked off, though there was no power outage.

Steve looked at me. "What's wrong?"

"In twenty minutes, your mom will call. Your great-grandmother has passed."

Twenty minutes later, the phone rang.

I can't explain these experiences through logic alone. They frightened me at the time, not because they were dark, but because they felt undeniably real. They confirmed other strange things I'd sensed before. Over time, they became part of a more profound awakening. Perhaps these moments were signs of something sacred. Or maybe they were meant to test the source of my gifts—whether divine or otherwise. Either way, they left no doubt; something beyond the ordinary was at work.

Through these supernatural happenings my confidence grew and reminded me that I had special gifts that I could use to help others. Now I needed to see if they were truly gifts from God or maybe an unworthy source.

Chapter 9

Spiritual Realization

While living in our apartment in Verdun, I befriended our neighbour, Armande St-Louis Powell, a widow with no children of her own. Our relationship began with a little gift. It was my birthday, and she left a gift bag with a birthday card and a present hanging on my doorknob. When I went to thank her we ended up sitting, chatting and having coffee. That was the start of our beautiful relationship.

At that time, she was 74 and I was in my early 20s. We connected and bonded; she became like the grandmother I never had, and likewise I was the granddaughter she never had. My grandparents died before I was born, and my father's mother died when I was a child.

Armande and I would often sit on the balcony, drinking coffee and talking. Whenever we had coffee, we would talk about life. She'd tell me stories about herself, and I told her mine. I could talk to her about anything and everything; she was trustworthy and made me feel safe.

One day while visiting, I noticed she had lost a lot of weight and she seemed to be fading away. I could tell just by looking at her eyes. I told her to ring our doorbell immediately if she felt off in any way.

A short while after she rang our doorbell, and we brought her to the hospital. The doctors performed some tests and discovered she had a tumour in her liver. She refused to receive any treatment. She had witnessed what chemotherapy had done to her brother (who had died from pancreatic cancer) and didn't want to suffer the same fate. "I'm 80 years old and don't want to go through all that," she told me.

While she was in the hospital, she showed me a locket her husband had given her. Engraved on it were the letters YT, which stood for "Yours Truly." Coincidentally, they were also my initials, Yolanda Tarantino. I don't believe in coincidences. She asked if I could go to her home, pack a bag for her and take care of her bird. She also instructed me to ensure her sisters didn't empty her belongings from the apartment before she passed.

She was in the hospital for two weeks before I received a call from her sister telling me Armande wasn't doing well, and the doctors did not give her much time to live. The day before her death, her sisters came and asked for the key to her apartment. There was nothing I could do but comply. Legally, they were her next of kin. They started to empty her house. While they were at her place, I decided to visit her at the hospital. But when I arrived, I was informed she had already passed away. Soon after that, one of her sisters called to provide the details of the funeral arrangements. Attending her funeral was the culminating point of my life.

As I walked towards her coffin to pay my respects, I saw Armande's spirit rise from her body. It was transparent, like the silhouettes of ghosts you see in movies. Her spirit hovered above her coffin. I let out a cry. My husband looked at me like I was a weirdo, but honestly I am convinced he would have reacted the same way. I told him I needed to go outside for some fresh air. Outside, I lit a cigarette to calm and compose myself.

While I stood there smoking, I could see the iron gates to the entrance of the cemetery, adjacent to the funeral home. Suddenly, I saw Armande's spirit appear in front of the gates. She waved at me, saying "Hello" and "Goodbye" at the same time. To her left a large window opened, where hundreds of thousands of small, bright, golden lights illuminated from within. She was then drawn through the window and became one of those flickers of golden light.

That was the first time I learned what happens to us after we pass from this world. We become this beautiful ball of light, almost like the flame of a candle. Armande went into this vortex of energy and became a beacon of light. That's when I knew without a doubt that we rise from death and go into other realms. This was the beginning of my study with spirituality and the afterlife.

Being at her service changed the direction of my life forever. Seeing her spirit that still hadn't ascended to Heaven was like seeing a translucent facsimile of who she was. That is the best way I can put it into words.

When Armande passed away, I was devastated; however, she left me with the revelation of where my future could lead me. She showed me where we go when we pass on. God always sends us the people we need in our lives when we need them. He sends them to help us heal, grow, and flourish.

From then on, many things became clear to me.

Chapter 10

Cultivating My Spiritual Gifts

I was happy that Armand was able to see my newborn son Ryan before she died. At 24, becoming a mother provided me with an even deeper level of connection with souls. During the second trimester I decided to take a nice, relaxing bath. I placed my hand on my stomach and asked my baby, "I wonder what you are going to be in life."

Suddenly, I felt my baby reply, telling me he would be a homosexual male. I was a little astonished. I wondered if this would be his path. I was also sad that he would choose such a challenging journey. A mother has a strong psychic connection with her fetus, a soul-to-soul connection. If you're open and willing, you can hear what your baby's soul has to say, as it is the soul that has chosen their mother.

After Ryan was born, I noticed signs from a young age that confirmed his revelation. He loved sparkly things. He wanted to play with dolls, and by the time he was four, he liked to put on my high heels and prance around. He identified with girlish things. Around the age of seven he would draw himself as a girl. I wondered if these little signs meant he might have been a woman in a past life. It could have also been a gender identity crisis.

With the help of a therapist at school, we let him choose what he wanted. It's truly up to the soul to decide for itself what lifestyle choices it wants. We can love and guide our children, but we can't choose or decide for them when it comes to what their soul truly wants.

Although I know the Bible has a traditional perspective on this, Jesus has always taught us not to judge, as he did when a crowd of men came to stone Mary of Magdalene to death. He did not defend or condemn her. He simply told those ready to stone her that if they were innocent of any sin in their lives, then they were welcome to throw a stone. Remember what happened? They all dropped their stones. When you use religion as an excuse to judge, condemn, or kill, then it becomes an ideology. Religion is meant to be a guide for love and respect towards everyone.

God Himself will judge—we just need to love everyone.

When The Spirit Speaks

The intuitive relationship I have with Ryan isn't merely a mother-child bond; I also have a strong connection with my husband.

When Ryan was three months old, my husband went out with some work friends for some drinks. Around one in the morning I gave my son his last feeding of the night and noticed my husband hadn't come home yet. As I was lying in bed I closed my eyes and saw the bar he was at, chatting with a server who had long black hair. In my vision, my husband was playing with his wedding band and ended up coming home late.

I snapped at him when he got home. "Where were you and why are you home so late? Did she have long black hair?"

Steve was shocked and told me everything. Steve went to a bar and the server was interested in him, wanting to meet up after her shift ended. His friend Denis saw what was happening and asked him, "Do you love your wife? If you love her, go home to her." When the server came back to their table, Steve turned her down and came home to me.

My second child, Mathew, was born three and a half years after Ryan. It was a difficult pregnancy, and the cord was wrapped twice around his neck. He stopped breathing, and the damage caused his Apgar score to read six. The Apgar score is a standardized assessment for infants immediately after delivery, based on their appearance, heart rate, reflexes, muscle tone, and respiration. Mathew was born with trauma from his first moment on Earth. When we brought him home, we noticed he was having breathing problems. We took him back to the hospital, and the doctors informed us that the mucus was getting stuck in his sinus, and he would probably snore even though he was a newborn.

Two months after Mathew's birth, Steve and I decided not to have any more children. I decided to have my tubes tied, yet I still felt like a third child might be in our future. Matthew was doing well until around 10 months, when he fell down the flight of stairs leading to the basement because my mother had accidentally left the door open. We took him to the hospital, and thankfully he had no broken bones. However, the shock of the fall had a neurological impact on him. It could have been so much worse. I don't even want to think about that. I believe an angel protected him from being severely harmed, as there was not a scratch on him.

When Ryan turned four, my mother asked if she could take him to a church-sponsored sleepaway camp. I was a little reluctant, and I asked her to reassure me that there were no bodies of water or boats close to or around the camp. She assured me there were none, so I let her take him.

As I was washing dishes in the kitchen, I suddenly saw a vision of Ryan flipping over in a canoe. I immediately panicked. As soon as the bus arrived, I lashed out at my mother. She was stunned and speechless. She was confused and wondered how I even knew what had happened. From that moment I never trusted my mother with my children again.

When you are open and willingly accept your gifts from God, the spirit will show you visions of what will happen to your loved ones. All these experiences and premonitions were signs of the gifts I possessed, and I wanted to learn more about them. How could I use these gifts to help others?

That summer, I wasn't feeling very well, having severe abdominal pains. One evening in July, my brother and I decided to go for a walk down by the LaSalle Rapids, a beautiful area by the St. Lawrence River. On the walk back home, I looked at the sky and saw a shooting star. My brother and I were very close at that time in our lives, and although my brother will never admit it, he also has special gifts of the spirit. I remember him turning to me and saying, "This shooting star was meant for you to see. Good things will happen in the future." Although they didn't happen right away, they would. Our sense of time and that of God are very different.

The next morning, I woke up in excruciating pain. I had been sleeping in the basement of our duplex and crawled up the stairs on my hands and knees. Though I was reluctant, I called my mother to come over to watch the kids. Since Steve worked nights, I had to wait for him to come home before he could take me to the hospital.

The staff performed blood work and informed me that I was pregnant and needed an emergency ultrasound. I was having an ectopic pregnancy and needed emergency surgery. I was fortunate that I got to the hospital in time, or it could have burst my fallopian tube. I didn't want to think about what could have happened.

After three days I returned home. I was supposed to rest, but how can you with two small children and a husband who worked nights? It was such a stressful time for me. My mother tried to help, but I felt alone and distanced from God. I was on autopilot. I did what I could and slowly recovered over the rest of the summer.

One night after I went to bed, I could see the moon shining through the window. As I drifted in and out of sleep, I looked up and saw purple, blue, and silver-coloured discs hovering above my body. I believed they were angels. I could hear voices speaking loudly, saying, "She's supposed to be asleep." They then flew out the window.

I ran up the flight of stairs so fast and slept on the couch in the living room and never slept in the basement again. The next morning I told Steve that we were going to move the bedroom into the living room, and move the living room downstairs. I refused to sleep another night in the basement.

In early spring 2000, I was feeling overwhelmed and exhausted. I needed a break, so I went to Puerto Vallarta with my mother-in-law and sister-in-law and took a week to rest. While I was there I met some lovely ladies from Alberta and Saskatchewan and spent some time with them. I told them a little about my psychic abilities, and they asked if I could perform a spiritual reading. It was the first time I ever attempted this. I used playing cards as a tool to concentrate and remember, telling one of the women that she was going to have a little girl who would be special.

At the end of the trip we exchanged contact information. We lost touch, however, years later one of the women managed to find me on Facebook to tell me that the spiritual reading I provided in Puerto Vallarta had manifested. She ended up having a daughter, which changed her in an incredibly profound way.

My 30s were a time when I learned and discovered a great deal about myself—they were truly eye-opening years. I did a lot of therapy, self-reflection, and became very aware and present. I was able to reflect and let go of things that blocked my emotional and spiritual growth.

The most important part was that I realized I had to deal with my issues. I couldn't blame others because they were also in pain and suffering. Through visualization exercises that I learned from a few of my therapies, I came to love and accept myself for who I was, and realized I didn't need to react to everything. I gave myself what I needed to keep moving forward. I stopped blaming others and took responsibility for the choices I made.

I decided to move from being a victim to self-empowered.

At 38, I finally had a life-altering discussion with my mother. She had been free of my father for a few years and had found her way back to God, becoming heavily involved with the Grace Church. She had worked on herself a lot as well. She ended up apologizing to me for not being present when I needed her. Although it was difficult to hear and accept, I took some comfort in her words. I had to forgive her, to let go of past resentments and anger and move past it all. I wanted a mother who would listen about how I had also been hurt and abused, but I could see I still did not have empathy, compassion, or the capacity to listen.

When I received God's gifts of the Spirit, one of the things the voice inside me said was that I would be able to know and see what came from God and what did not. At times, I feel it's a blessing and other times, a curse. But I have come to accept it for what it is. But I know no matter what, God protects me.

"God is my Refuge. The one who lives in the shelter of the Most High, who rests in the shadow of the Almighty will say to the LORD, you are my refuge, my fortress, and my God in whom I trust. He will surely deliver you from the hunter's name and from the destructive plague. With his feathers he

will cover you under his wings; you will find safety. His truth is your shield and your armour. You need not fear the terror that stalks in the night nor the arrow that flies in the day, nor the plague that strikes in the darkness or calamity that destroys at noon. If a thousand fall at your side or ten thousand at your right hand, it will not overcome you. Only observe it with your eyes and you will see how the wicked are paid back. LORD you are my refuge. Because you chose the Most High as your dwelling place, no evil will fall upon you, and no affliction will approach your tent for he will command his angels to protect you in all your ways, with their hands they will lift you up so you will not trip over a stone, you will stomp on lions and snakes, you will trample the young lions and serpents. Because he has focused his love on me. I will deliver him. I will protect him. Because he knows my name. When he calls out to me, I will answer him. I will be with him in his distress, I will deliver him, and I will honour him. I will satisfy him with a long life. I will show him my deliverance."

(Psalm 91)

Chapter 11

Healing From Within

Over the years I experienced chronic health problems, particularly with my ovaries and uterus. My periods were excruciating, often leaving me bedridden for a week every month. I carried constant abdominal and back pain. Looking back, I now understand how the emotional and psychological scars of my past, especially the trauma I had suppressed, were manifesting in my physical body.

Emotional pain doesn't just live in the mind—it settles into the flesh. Panic attacks, anxiety, and depression accompanied my buried trauma. My physical issues were linked to the first chakra, which governs sexuality, security, and safety. I was diagnosed with ovarian cysts and uterine fibroids—clear signs that my body was crying out for help. I had been pushing through life, suppressing emotions, always moving, never stopping to feel.

In 1991, I worked for the military, which had been contracted to decontaminate a World War II site north of Montreal. The terrain was rugged and overgrown. One day I joked about a body being buried in a disturbed patch of ground. Moments later, a human hand was found exactly where I pointed. The police were called. To this day I believe a spirit had imprinted that message on my mind. Later that same day, I fell into a trench and injured my back. I never returned to that job.

Despite two years of physical therapy, the pain persisted. An orthopedic surgeon finally listened, ran appropriate tests, and in 1992, I had my first surgery to remove the nucleus pulposus found on my spinal disc at L4-L5. The relief was immense. I could finally consider pregnancy without unbearable pain. A second back surgery followed in 1993, where rods and screws were inserted.

I remember waking up after the surgery and seeing my mother by my bedside. The first thing I blurted out was everything about my sexual abuse from my childhood. She was shocked and initially thought I was delirious from the anesthetics. In speaking with a professional at the hospital, she learned that when people are under anesthesia and wake up, repressed memories from a deep trauma can resurface. My mother now understood why I had become so withdrawn and never wanted to be left alone anywhere without her. And most importantly, why I didn't trust anyone.

The Soul's Awakening: Spiritual Insight and Emotional Healing

Therapy helped me uncover how deeply the abuse had impacted every part of me. My therapist quickly saw that my pain was more than physical. Making the connection between past trauma and present suffering changed my life. In my late twenties I finally began the real work of healing. Rebuilding trust after abuse is slow and painful, but essential. It's also spiritual.

Healing requires spiritual openness. Every illness carries an emotional root. The body reflects our inner wounds. When we open ourselves to prayer, to the Holy Spirit, to awareness of the Divine within, healing begins. Christ consciousness for me means having the mind of Christ—seeing with compassion, truth, and grace.

It wasn't until my late 20s that I was finally able to start working on my issues and heal myself. It was a time of growth. When a person is sexually abused their basic feeling of trust is broken. Learning to trust again took a considerable amount of time. I had to relearn how to trust people and let people in. What many people don't realize is that negative entities can attach themselves to a person's aura. When you are broken and are angry towards God, you are turning away from God, allowing the negative entities to find you.

Every challenge we experience in our physical body is associated with emotional trauma. Our body manifests disturbances in our emotions and spirit. It is crucial to pray, listen, and understand what our body is trying to communicate to us. When you are born again, experience nirvana, or are aware of the spirit, God is at work in you.

When the Holy Spirit comes upon us, God has sent us the advocate as He promised. When I speak about Christ consciousness, I speak about having the mind of Christ as we go about our lives. The Holy Spirit exposes the truth about all things. The beauty of this is that we have the opportunity to work on ourselves throughout our entire lives, regardless of how challenging, traumatic, devastating, or detrimental it may be—we can overcome anything in our lives through the grace of God.

Whenever God sends the Holy Spirit upon me, there are moments I feel so much joy in my heart and other moments when I am filled with the deepest of sorrow and tears, and sometimes I laugh excessively. I realize that God has always been present in my life in some shape or form even though I haven't always been able to recognize His presence. In hindsight, I can now see when and how He was present.

All of my spiritual gifts and works in conjunction with all the professional help I've received over the years, allowed for a total healing transformation. Essentially, when you are connected through your heart with the mind of Christ and go within, allowing yourself to merge with the Divine Spirit, the sickness in your body that needs healing is revealed. God will remove your shortcomings, and you will be completely healed.

In native culture, a shaman believes good and bad spirits have their own ritual. They believe the Spirit reveals things to all people through their medicine. The Spirit allows people to discern for themselves what truth is revealed. We need to be open to the world and welcome what it has to offer us. If we don't stop the vicious cycle of repeating patterns, whether it be negative patterns we learned from our parents or patterns we created ourselves, that's when disease can set in and we become sick and stop evolving. We don't learn the lesson that's been provided to us. When we finally decide to stop repeating those patterns and move forward, that's when true healing sets in.

Sometimes, the way God tries to get our attention can be ironic; He has a strange sense of humour. Sometimes our bodies must come to a complete stop to get our attention. Our body has such profound wisdom, and it lets us know when it is in pain or has experienced emotional trauma, such as sexual abuse. Sometimes, our spirit can even leave the body to protect itself.

Becoming Whole: Tools, Practices, and Lifelong Growth

I've had many clients and friends who have come to me for energy healing. I have worked with clients who experienced such traumatic experiences that they were not connected to their physical bodies at all. My experience of being sexually abused and learning to cultivate empathy and compassion allows me to connect with the energies of other people. I can sense people who are suffering emotionally, even those who have yet to manifest any physical signs.

If you think about it carefully, when your life is in chaos, where do you learn about love? Through God! God created you in His image, a spiritual being living in a physical body, and loves you unconditionally. God helped me to parent myself because my parents didn't know what they were doing. Everyone is doing the best they can within their limits, and some are more limited than others.

There is always hope on the horizon, and it requires us to step out of our comfort zone and go beyond what we have been taught. To grow we need to plant seeds for our souls. Prayer is powerful because of its energy, cleansing, healing, and breaking of generational curses, and deliverance through Jesus Christ from dark spirits or negative forces.

Providing spiritual guidance to people can be tricky and challenging for those who are not ready to accept it or require proof to validate the truth. One thing I've learned on my journey is to work and heal through the chakras. I learned how to heal my affected chakras, primarily my first and second chakras, which are connected to my sense of security, sexual organs, and lower back.

An excellent exercise is breathing. It can help us connect our heart, mind, and spirit. I also emphasize how much laughter is the best medicine for healing. By taking Reiki courses and reading the book *Hands of Light* by Barbara Ann Brennan, I came to understand that we are energy, and due to negative personal experiences, our energy can become trapped. As healers, we tend to attract people who are trapped, who have suffered as we have.

It also works in reverse. Through spiritual readings, I would sometimes even have contact with departed loved ones who were abusers. For example, a father who had abused their child in some form and as a consequence they were stuck in their realm. They could not move forward because the child was not able to forgive and let go. Healing also occurs in the spiritual realm just as it does in the physical realm, through the power of forgiveness and letting go.

A crucial concept to understand is that you must continually work on yourself.

I still work on myself, crucially the connection between our body, mind, and spirit. Over the past 20 years, I have worked extensively on my issues using different forms of healing and still continue to heal, even to this day. Life is a living, breathing experience in which we need to always be mindful and present. We need to listen to our bodies. We must be conscious of what triggers us. The emotional trauma we experience affects our human soul on many levels. We start by peeling away at the layers of emotional trauma we have experienced. I had to do this to understand how my emotional trauma and abuse affected my relationships with my family and friends.

My goal is to become whole and love all of myself, even the damaged parts. And I have to note that I do not look at myself from a victim's perspective. I can grieve about what happened in the past and learn to love myself while using it as a means of self-empowerment. I've learned to recognize that everything is an outside influence, and I have the power to decide how I choose to react to those external situations. Only you can decide the difference you want to make in your own life.

My thirst to heal has no limits. There are several different methodologies one can use to help them on their journey. There is not only one way to heal, nor is there only one recipe for everyone. Sometimes it is the combination of many tools that allows us to heal. I've engaged in various types of therapies to help me through my traumatic experiences. I have done therapy sessions with psychologists. I have had acupuncture. I have worked with healers and received body massages and reflexology treatments. I've also had Reiki sessions and learned how to perform self-healing, which is part of the first level of Reiki training.

Reiki holds a special place in my heart because it heals through the use of the universal life force's energies. It helps move stagnant energy and bring it into the open, allowing it to heal. All of these methods of healing work on the energies of the body, where different meridians relate to a specific organ, and they all work together to help becoming a whole individual. This sort of energetic work helped me understand who I am as a soul and how to better myself overall. I've learned to listen to my body and to love all aspects of who I am, the dark parts of me, as well as the light ones. After all, we are multifaceted humans. We are complex creatures. We can choose the energy we need to create the life that we want. Every person responds differently to various types of therapy. It's important you find the ones that can help you heal the best.

Through my own experience, you can see how disease and emotional trauma affect the physical body. In John 15:1-8:

> "I am the true vine, and my Father is the gardener. He cuts off every branch in me that bears no fruit, while every branch that does bear fruit, he prunes so that it will be even more fruitful. You are already clean because of the words I have spoken to you. Remain in me, as I also remain in you. No branch can bear fruit by itself; it must remain in the vine. Neither can you bear fruit unless you remain in me."

Through all my pain and suffering and healing, I now understand that God was pruning me. I used my abuse as a crutch, an addiction to cope. I kept looking outside of myself instead of looking within. It's not until I experienced these health issues that I was forced to stop and try to understand why I was in so much pain. There were times I couldn't even get out of bed. Despite all this, I persisted.

God had been trying to reach out during my times of crisis, but I never paid attention. I was a vine that he was trying to prune, but I couldn't recognize the signs. Being sick forced me to calm my mind and begin to tap into my consciousness. At first it was barely 30 seconds, then it became one minute. I don't know how long I have been able to stay in a state of complete consciousness, but it's not the length of time that matters; it's the healing that happens during the practice.

Chapter 12

Greg

It was not until I met Greg that I began my true spiritual transition. Greg was a wonderful man whom God sent to cross my path and guided me on my journey to become a spiritual healer. I met Greg and his wife, Danielle (Danny), through my husband Steve, who were friends from their military days. We all hit it off right away.

Greg and I had many things in common, but the most important was our deep hunger to learn about God, Jesus, and the Bible. We spoke openly about the Bible and my spiritual gifts.

When you looked at Greg, you would have never thought he was studying to become a reverend. His appearance was quite deceiving in the sense that he was a six-feet-four-inch-tall man with beautiful blue eyes. He taught martial arts and owned a successful security training school in Montreal, and was highly interested in the spiritual side of life. When you think of a reverend, he's not exactly the image that comes to mind. Greg was a deeply layered person—strong in presence, yet soft in spirit. At the time, he had been living with his girlfriend, Danny, who would eventually become his third wife. She was supportive of his spiritual life and showed great interest in spiritual readings.

One day, I read for Danny and commented that there would be a time when she would be staying at home instead of working. She looked at me, confused. She was a hard worker and worked alongside Greg at his security business. The reason wasn't understood during the reading, and it wasn't until years later that it revealed itself. She ended up stopping work and staying at home so she could care for her husband, who was fighting a life-threatening illness.

Greg had been struck with a rare type of cancer, located in the bile duct by the liver. Over time, the doctors operated and removed his gallbladder, and he also had follow-up chemo treatments.

Faith, Healing, and The Golden Cross Vision

Before cancer, I learned that Greg's dream was to have his own ministry, and that dream came to fruition at The Church of Christian Discovery. He became a deacon with the Anglican church and a pastor in Lancaster, Ontario. Sometimes I would accompany him, and as we drove we would discuss spirituality and dig deeply into my visions. Little did I know how Greg would affect me.

I joined Greg's church as a worker and was baptized by being submerged in a sink full of water. Danny would be the witness and videotaped the baptism to be put on VHS. I know that dates me!

As Greg recited the words, "Do you accept Jesus Christ as your saviour?" the room lit up, and the kitchen window over the sink filled with an indescribable, almost supernatural light... and it was all caught on camera. I accepted Jesus Christ as my saviour.

At the time of Greg's illness, I was studying Reiki and learning how to heal with my hands. Reiki can be used in conjunction with any other method of healing, as it enhances and works to balance and restore the body's equilibrium. It is also suitable for plants and animals. Prayer intends to ask for healing in Jesus' name for the person who needs it, whether for physical illness or spiritual restoration.

Greg had no time to waste and readily agreed to become my test subject. Between chemo treatments, he would sometimes come to my place, and I would put on some healing music. I would often use a beautiful medley of music called "The Silent Path." When I placed my hands over a particular area of his body, I would frequently feel my spirit leave my body and sense the spiritual beings around me, helping me to heal him.

On one particular day, Greg asked me for a healing and my husband drove me over. As we entered the basement, I could see that through the huge bay window the skies were overcast despite the gorgeous day. Greg was sitting in his La-Z-Boy, listening to his correspondence course on the Bible. He was always in a pleasant mood, brave and fighting the good fight.

I joined Greg in listening to the Bible verses. We discussed his healing and its progress. I had my hands on his stomach above his scar. I could feel the energy making my hands very hot. When I perform spiritual healing with my hands, they either become very hot or very cold. In Reiki, you can place your hands on the body or hover above it.

With my hands on his stomach, suddenly three beautiful beams of golden light spread across his belly. We looked up, and on one of the beams there was an exquisite golden cross that looked like a star. It was one of the most breathtaking visions I'd ever witnessed. Steve slept through the entire thing. It was not meant for him to witness, it was only meant for Greg and I.

When Greg witnessed this beautiful cross, he asked: "Is what I'm seeing real?" Ah, Greg, my beloved doubting Thomas. In the New Testament, Jesus' disciple Thomas didn't believe Jesus had risen until he placed his fingers in the holes in Jesus' hand where he had been nailed to the cross.

Although Greg was very religious, he was always searching for concrete proof. I would always tell him, "In order for you to believe, you need to see it for yourself, don't you?" and he would laugh. Blessed are those who believe without proof—that is true faith. I used to tell him he would get his proof one day, and on that day he did! This magnificent golden cross that shone amongst the darkness of that gloomy day with a blinding light so bright no one could look at it—that was his final proof.

When the vision appeared, I received a message. The message told me that because Greg was so devoted to God and reading the Bible, God was letting him know of His presence. "Greg, you're getting your miracle. Here is your proof. God is sending you this beautiful cross of light hovering over us. God is saying, 'I am here.'"

The light stayed with us the entire time I worked on his stomach. I was happy to share this beautiful moment with him—the miracle of God's existence.

Faith Beyond Death: The Cross, The Spirit, and Eternal Hope

Sadly, on May 11th, 2004, Greg succumbed to cancer, and the Lord brought him home. Greg's passing was very sad. I've always wondered what seeing the cross meant for him. Did he take it as a sign that God would heal his cancer? or a more profound understanding, that his time on earth was coming to an end and God was waiting for him with open arms? Was the cancer his cross to bear on this earth before meeting God? No matter what it was, it was a sign he was going to move into the next phase of his life and be with God.

Greg often asked me about my perspective on the spirit world. The spirit transitions from this plane to the next, and we keep evolving. On the other hand, Greg believed there was an end, which led to Heaven. He didn't necessarily believe we rose from death.

He told me, "If we can roam around after we die and visit our loved ones, then I will come and visit you. I will touch you behind your head and you'll know it's me."

Two years after he passed, I still hadn't felt his presence. I often thought of him and prayed for him, but I received no spiritual contact from him. I wanted so badly to feel his presence. From my understanding, when someone passes under traumatic or intense circumstances, the spirit crosses over and sometimes remains in a cocoon-like state. For us, it might seem like the cocooning process takes a long time, but for those who have crossed over, time is irrelevant. A year could be a millisecond. The spirit of the departed has to return and learn to be a spirit again. At this point, I let go of any expectations and allowed the natural process to unfold without anxious anticipation. Everything unfolds with the ebb and flow of the universe, always on God's time, not ours. And then it happened.

One night while lying in bed next to my sleeping husband, I felt someone touch me at the back of my head. I looked over at Steve, who was curled up under the blankets on the other side of the bed. It startled me. Had I imagined it? I used logic and ruled out the fact that it couldn't have been Steve; he was asleep. A voice in my head said, "Hi. It's me. I told you I would come visit and I would touch your head. Sorry, it took so long."

It was such a monumental and beautiful moment, I laughed out loud. Greg was a doubter, but now? His presence reassured and strengthened my faith, encouraging me to keep moving forward.

Greg believed that seeing the cross was his reassurance that his story would be told through me to bring about God's glory. It meant Jesus was with him through all his suffering. In that beautiful golden cross it appeared as if Jesus was telling Greg, "I am with you. You are not alone. Give me all your suffering."

We all live different experiences, and there are various ways to perceive death, the supernatural, and spirituality. One of my goals is to show those who have had similar experiences as Greg that they are not alone. They are not crazy. I want this book to help them feel validated in their truth.

We need to start our journey by allowing the light of Jesus to shine upon us and let it be a beacon of light within us. I realized that Greg's vision reminded me of the truth of the Bible, where Jesus is described as the light of the world.

As Scripture reminds us in John 14:6

> "I am the way and the truth and the life. No one comes to the Father except through me. If you really know me, you will know my Father as well."

The vertical line of the cross is the divine communication with God, whereas the horizontal aspect is where God's consciousness pours out. That is what the divine communication through Christ to the Father is when he comes down to us. When we take matters into our own hands, we get the results we get. Our resources and our reach are limited. However, when we leave things in God's hands and His doing, He will surpass all human conditioning, expectations, and understanding. He provides us with a more miraculous result because He isn't limited.

Where man fails, God succeeds!

I have contemplated the vision of the golden cross and considered what Christ's journey must have been like when He was crucified. He bore all our sins, our pain, our demons and paid the ultimate price for us so we could be saved. His behaviour and teachings allowed us to embrace the Spirit of God. Through Jesus, we received spiritual renewal; we were born again. Jesus also left his advocate, the Holy Spirit, so we are never alone.

When we are reborn in the Spirit, we are in union with Christ and our heavenly Father. The Holy Spirit becomes our teacher and guide, helping us to live in the spirit of Jesus and not as the old Adamic man. Jesus did away with the old sinful Adam of the Old Testament and ushered the world into a new doctrine. We are now brothers and sisters in Christ and not the wicked descendants of Adam and Eve. Jesus came to give us a new way, and because of his sacrifice we no longer need to atone for our sins. We were made clean. We were freed.

It was so important for me to tell you about the beautiful golden cross of Jesus I saw with Greg. Through all the pain and suffering in my life, I had never felt so loved or wanted. Jesus Christ saved me, setting me free. He gave me peace in the knowledge that he loves me.

Whenever I think of Jesus, I often think of the song by Sinead O'Connor, "Nothing Compares to You." For me, nothing in this world compares to Christ and our Father in heaven. When I am absent from my spiritual union with Christ, I feel lost and disconnected. When I am connected to Christ and God, I feel whole, happy, and at peace. Those are the moments when we heal, grow, and evolve. We evolve through the school of life to become the best versions of ourselves as humans.

That is how we are anointed by the Spirit.

It is said plainly in John 4:23-24, "*Yet the time is coming, and is now here, when true worshippers will worship the Father in Spirit and Truth. Indeed, the Father is looking for people like that to worship him. God is Spirit, and those who worship him must worship in Spirit and Truth.*"

Chapter 13

Lyn and René

In December 2003, I attended a spiritual tea at the Spiritual Healing church, founded in 1964 by Charles and Janette Grayden. They were spiritualists from England who had immigrated to Canada and started their spiritual church in Montreal. In 1980, they handed the church over to Gilles and Michael Morin. The Spiritual Healing church is a non-profit organization whose mission is to serve others spiritually. The church has received numerous prophetic words of wisdom and experienced spiritual healing through prayer and spiritual energy for over 50 years.

Spiritual tea is a meeting with a medium of your choice, and is how I first met Lyn Boucher and her husband, René. The couple used to work at psychic and metaphysical fairs in Montreal, and coincidentally, I remembered taking a flyer when I passed by their booth once. I had set the flyer aside without realizing our paths would cross again 20 years later. During our first meeting, Lyn told me that my aura was of the colour purple, which represents high spirituality. She also told me I had an open third eye and a crown chakra, which is also indicative of higher intuition.

Lyn was a beautiful spirit—a spiritual teacher, clairvoyant, author, energy and spiritual healer, reverend, and well-versed in trance mediumship. She was tough but fair, all while standing at only five feet tall. Her philosophy was that everyone should have the chance to learn how to become a better person. She was loved by all those who knew her. She was selfless and devoted her life to serving a higher purpose. Lyn was but one of the many precious people who have gone through the doors of the Spiritual Healing church.

Lyn and René helped me further develop my ability to sense and perceive spirits who have passed on or those transitioning into the light. It wasn't all a dream; this was all very real. I had a talent and needed to acknowledge, develop, and utilize the gifts God had given me.

In 2004, shortly after Greg's passing, I began taking classes with Lyn and René and started my work in healing and spiritual readings. The timing could not have been more appropriate. Life was guiding me, and everything was falling into place. Greg was the start, and Lyn and René were the continuation of the journey into my gifts. Through the gifts of the spirit, I was able to connect my soul to another's soul and its energy.

Being part of this spiritual community helped me discover my true path, which led to becoming an interfaith minister —a minister in service to people of all faiths and those with no faith. The church and my faith helped me evolve my spiritual gifts and to meditate correctly. It provided me with the stability and credibility I was seeking. It allowed me to connect with others like myself, who also had questions and were seeking the truth about the supernatural.

When I started Lyn's classes, I had a dream about her during one of her meditation classes. She and I were walking down a road together with a few other students from our class, and she led us to a beautiful water well. As I looked in the well, the water shone like a mirror, and I could see my reflection. Suddenly, I snapped out of the meditation. I eventually came to understand that this dream showed me she was going to lead the way, and I needed to follow her to find and understand my true calling. For me, God is like the well; once you drink from it, you transform, and He will spiritually make you thirst no more.

Whenever Lyn and I had counselling sessions, she would see how determined I was trying to find my path while being true to myself. The most important thing she would say to me was to be specific and stop dancing around a topic. Lovingly, she would force me to look deep within myself and be truthful about what I wanted. She never judged me and became like a spiritual mother to me.

Her husband, René, enjoyed sitting on the second floor of our church. He would sit in an old chair, which he nicknamed 'Mom's chair' because it was the favourite sitting spot of Reverend Gilles Morin's mother, a woman who many people loved and respected in the church. Many people adopted her as their second mom, hence the name, Mom's chair. René had this unique way of talking about his life experience in the third person. He would provide these subtle sayings, like whispers, that have stayed with me.

The truth is, I didn't want to let go of the anger from my youth because I had judgments and opinions about them. To counter this, René suggested I read a few books. He gave me an international bestseller, *The Four Agreements*, by Miguel Ruiz. René would have me examine a situation and encourage me to reflect on my thoughts and processes while reading these inspirational books. I realized that to become whole, I had to change my mindset. One of the most extraordinary things I learned from René is to be all that I can be. When I talked about finding a place to belong, I didn't have to look any further. I had seen it.

I realized I could be so much more. Through meditation and visualization, I was able to heal my mind and body and change the images that have haunted me. I was able to dissipate the thoughts that oppressed and kept me down. I learned how to rise above everything and find inner peace, as well as to forgive those who wronged me. I was able to let go of the anger and allow God to fill my heart with love.

Between 2004 to 2006, I continued my journey and studies towards becoming a reverend. During one meditation session I had a spiritual vision. It felt like my spirit had left my body, leading me to a staircase in a magnificent room where an ample, beautiful open flame stood, like the Olympic flame. As I was taking in the beauty of this room, someone placed a torch in my hands and a voice said to me, "You were chosen." I believe it meant to continue passing on the knowledge I was learning.

Sadly, René Boucher passed away in 2011. Sometimes I feel his energy, and whenever I do, tears always come to my eyes. A few years later, on March 27th, 2016 (also Easter Sunday), I had a dream in which I was with a group of people who seemed familiar, and I realized they were my spirit guides. Then someone placed an emerald tablet in my hands. I woke up with a massive headache. I didn't feel quite like myself. However, I sat in meditation, allowing my thoughts to come and go, and then went about my day.

At 9 am, I received a phone call from my friend and mentor, Reverend Gilles Morin. He informed me that my spiritual teacher, mentor, and friend, Reverend

Lyn, had passed away early that morning. I took this as a sign that I had been given the tablet of truth to carry on the work Lyn had begun.

My life changed from that moment, as I had a beautiful gift. A gift which allowed me to pass on the knowledge I had obtained to others and share the gifts of the Spirit. After Lyn's passing, I became more involved in my church. I began teaching my spiritual classes and became a licensed minister, as well as a reverend, certified by the government of Quebec. I can perform weddings, funerals, baptisms, and naming ceremonies. In addition to my daily responsibilities, I continue to provide spiritual readings and church services.

Lyn would often make her presence known. It always felt like this little source of energy on my left shoulder blade, and other times on my right. It's a spiralling feeling, a light tingle of energy flowing to that area. And every time it happens, it brings me a sense of peace and reminds me that I am never alone.

Lyn and René were both relentless lightworkers who are now stars in Heaven—individuals in their own way, yet still shining bright. Simply put, lightworkers can see everything in the light of God, the infinite omnipresent energy from which we come and return to. We bring love to the world in the face of darkness and fear. We feel a strong urge to help others. Lightworkers volunteer to act as a beacon for the Earth and commit themselves to serving humanity.

Though it has been over a decade since they passed, it feels like only yesterday I was with them.

Their departure has left a deep mark on my soul. I always feel it whenever I deal with death; it's like a million needles entering my body. My insides cried for a very long time for both of them.

I believe God placed both of them on my path so I could learn from them, and I am forever grateful to Him for them. They gave me so much spiritual "bread," and I now find myself doing what they did for me for others.

They are my two guiding stars, encouraging me to go on. They both guide me spiritually, inspire and provide me with messages to help me along my spiritual journey. They are always by my side, moving forward with me so I can be of service to others.

Chapter 14

The Journey To Enlightenment

A s I wrote in a previous chapter, one of the turning points in my life was when I saw the spirit of Armande St. Louis Powell turn into a glowing flame of light after her passing. This experience allowed me to accept all the other experiences I have witnessed. It allowed me to come to understand the gifts of the Spirit and how they had been whispering to me, enabling my quest for the truth.

What exactly does it mean to be enlightened? Enlightenment means being free from ignorance and misinformation. I decided to further enrich my knowledge by taking courses that would enable me to evolve as a truth seeker. God and all the people He placed on my path were leading me towards various learning tools, courses, and other studies. We attract that which we seek, similar to what we have heard about the law of attraction. We are energy, and we can manifest our thoughts when we focus on what we truly want or need. I would eventually come to learn that, despite all my studies, experiences, and healings, the actual truth is that God is Spirit, and we are all connected to Him. Through this understanding, I felt enlightened.

Growing up, Christianity shaped my beliefs, and more specifically, Catholicism. As I evolved in life I became very open to learning about other religions and traditions, as I wanted others to perceive me as an open-minded person. I wanted to make sure I didn't come across as authoritative or controlling. I sought to understand my ideological stance concerning the Catholic Church, as I was baptized into that religion. Were my experiences compatible with the ideology of Catholicism?

Not only that, but I wanted to study comprehensively to appreciate a broader perspective, from different angles. I even learned about the occult and New Age—anything that could help me, as I was hungry for knowledge and understanding.

I want people to realize that although we are born into a religion, it's okay to identify the flaws within that religion and not willingly accept everything you hear. I firmly believe that we are constantly evolving; we need to continually educate ourselves, be open to learning new things, and test and verify the truth of what is good.

Exploring Energetic Healing and Spiritual Modalities

As part of my quest for knowledge, I decided to learn Reiki. Reiki was the first form of energy healing I learned. There are specific points and organs in the body where you can help release stagnant energy to improve the overall flow within the body. Reiki also allows you to heal a person from a distance or even perform healing on yourself.

I studied the chakra system, which also focuses on the body's energy. It helped me have a deeper understanding of how we are all spiritual beings. I learned that it is crucial to be balanced and to feel from the inside out, a process I am still developing. Being emotional beings, everything is connected—our mind, body, and spirit.

I have also studied cranial therapy with Dr. Fidel Beeman in Montreal. Cranial therapy is a powerful healing tool in understanding how our bones have energy. Level 1 of the program allowed me to know how our skeletal system informs us of who we are. While studying cranial therapy, I received a spiritual message that makes me believe that all the DNA of our past continues to live in our bones.

Not only that, I am a Qigong instructor in the making, taking a course with Master Lee Holden, who is well-known in the United States and has an online program. Qigong teaches you about specific acupressure points, where the meridians in the body are located and how to massage to activate them. Qigong teaches you how to transform stagnant energy into health and vitality.

Being present and being quiet is a way for us to learn to become whole. One insightful book I read was *A Guide to Healing Through the Human Energy Field* by Barbara Brennan. It teaches you how the body is a vessel of energy and what you can do with that energy field.

When I was younger I dabbled a little in Tarot cards, which is considered New Age; however, I have come to understand there is a difference between psychic and spirit energy. I initially used the Tarot cards to build credibility, as people needed something more concrete. As I continued to follow the path of spirits, I developed beyond Tarot cards. It was quite a process for me to learn a tool commonly used in fortune-telling. You have to be very careful with energies and the types of energy you work with.

Over time, during any Tarot readings, I was receiving messages from spirit guides, but I came to realize that the cards were not contributing to the reading. Although it was a useful tool to get me started, in the end it didn't serve my higher purpose. People were relying solely on what they believed the cards had to say, rather than on my gifts. I was using the cards to ensure people believed me because I was not confident enough in my own abilities. It was there as a tangible resource as some people had a hard time believing unless there was something physical they could see.

I was doing readings based on my abilities and not because of the cards.

As time went on, I realized Tarot readings were not an energy that represented God; they represented something that was not of God. And instead of moving towards God, a voice told me I was moving towards the occult, and that Tarot cards were not good and offensive to God. The voice said to me that because I was still in my rebellious stage, evil spirits were trying to place me under the illusion that it was ok and acceptable to God, when in fact it was not. I decided to make changes and turn towards the word of God as my tool instead of Tarot cards. In reading the Bible, I also came upon an affirmation of this.

In Deuteronomy 18:10-12: *"There shall not be found among you any one that maketh his son or his daughter to pass through the fire, or that useth divination, or an observer of times, or an enchanter, or a witch. Or a charmer, or a consulter with familiar spirits, or a wizard, or a necromancer. For all that do these things are an abomination unto the Lord: and because of these abominations the Lord thy God doth drive them out from before thee. Thou shalt be perfect with the Lord thy God."*

All the meditation classes I've taken over the past 20 years have helped me focus and quiet my mind, allowing me to be present. During my reverential studies, I also realized my greater purpose was to serve my community and to be a servant of God. All the various courses were a way for me to come to terms with who God was in my life.

The Call to Purpose:
From Spiritual Curiosity to Divine Direction

After giving birth to my second son, Matthew, I developed a deep interest in spirituality. The first book I ever read on my journey was *Ask Your Angels: A Practical Guide to Working with the Messengers of Heaven to Empower and Enrich Your Life,* by Alma Daniel, Timothy Wyle, and Andrew Ramer. I stumbled upon it browsing in the La Salle Library, and I know it wasn't by accident.

I was asking God what my higher purpose was, and came face-to-face with this book. This book had everything I needed and was looking for, and most importantly, it revolved around angels.

The book included exercises on how to sit quietly and meditate, as well as how to ask for guidance from higher levels of spiritual beings or God's helpers. I believe that from a very young age I always had angelic support, but was not aware of it until later in life. In the upheaval of my childhood I was constantly searching for an identity. All the supernatural occurrences I experienced in my childhood helped me discover, identify, and solidify my true calling. This ultimately led me to become a reverend, doing so in a spiritual and healing way by bridging the gap between the physical and non-physical realms.

When you get in touch with God through Christ, you become renewed. The number one guide is to listen to your spirit, which will reveal the truth. You need to listen to your inner voice. The Holy Spirit within you will tell the truth about all matters. It will only use what's good for you to develop strength, courage, perseverance, and vanquish fear.

Once you know the enemy, you know how to deal with them. When you develop discernment, you learn to conquer fear. To be honest, even when I was studying everything, it didn't satisfy my soul. It didn't fill all the gaps.

It was not until I made a genuine connection with God through Christ that I truly understood who I was.

Chapter 15

The Anointing of the Spirit

The first time the Holy Spirit descended onto humans was at Pentecost. This event has evolved into a Christian holiday celebrated on the 50th day after Easter Sunday. Pentecost commemorates the moment the Holy Spirit came upon the Apostles and other followers of Jesus Christ while they were in Jerusalem for the Feast of Weeks, as described in the Acts of the Apostles.

Acts 2:1-4 describes the fulfillment of Pentecost, where the early Christians first received the outpouring of the Holy Spirit. *"And when the day of Pentecost was fully come, they were all with one accord in one place. And suddenly there came a sound from heaven as of a rushing mighty wind, and it filled all the house where they were sitting. And there appeared unto them cloven tongues like as of fire, and it sat upon each of them. And they were all filled with the Holy Ghost, and began to speak with other tongues, as the Spirit gave them utterance."*

One night, my brother, Angelo, was over at my house and we had a small argument about his excessive drinking. It left me feeling upset. Although we are not close, I still love him regardless of our differences because he's my little brother. That night, he seemed to be a little more receptive to the idea of negative energies that follow us and how we all have inner demons. He was tired of fighting this compulsion and disease of drinking and felt that maybe, just maybe, outside forces were working against him.

Inner demons can take the form of addictions, usually due to unresolved or unfinished issues in a person's life. And those issues can turn into dangerous addictions if they are not dealt with properly. It frightened Angelo because he normally suppresses any spiritual feelings through the use of alcohol. That night, he felt like he might be under attack and wanted to make amends. I told Angelo he should consult with someone to resolve his drinking addiction.

After he left, I sat under the porch light and held my Bible. I have my Bible near when I feel I need guidance, solace, or comfort. At that moment I was hurting for my brother. I closed my eyes and had a vision of a man wearing sandals standing in the sand. He wore a robe, but I couldn't see his face. He then blew me a swirl of energy, saying,

"I give you the gift of prophecy. I give you the gift of healing. I give you the gift of teaching. I give you the gift to know what comes from God and which does not."

Then he blew the breath of the Holy Spirit three times on me. These were the same gifts that the Bible mentions in Corinthians 1:7-11:

"But the manifestation of the Spirit is given to each one for the profit of all, for to one is given the word of wisdom through the Spirit, to another the word of knowledge through the same Spirit, to another faith by the same Spirit, to another the gift of healing by the same Spirit, to another the working of miracles, to another prophecy, to another discerning of spirits, to another different kinds of tongues, to another the interpretation of tongues. But the same Spirit works all these things, distributing to each one individually as He wills all the spiritual gifts will not come unless you have love in your heart."

I opened my eyes and thought I must have been tripping, but I don't do drugs, at least, not since I was a teenager. I couldn't believe what I saw or felt. I became more open to the gifts bestowed upon me. However, the gifts were not enough. I also felt the need to establish my credibility. It was vital for me to have something to fall back on in case this was all a figment of my imagination.

People may not always like the messages I provide, as the truth forces them to look deeply within themselves and make the decision to heal that which no longer serves their higher purpose. My goal is to be there to help, bring healing, and guide any person who wants to become whole and unite with the Spirit of God.

I was sitting and reflecting deeply, and it became very clear to me that I needed to emphasize all of my supernatural experiences in this book, especially my relationship with the Spirit of God, to help people understand what it is to have a union with God. I want to:

- Help you understand what it means to be born again and renewed.
- Help you understand what it means to leave behind your desires, your egos, your sins of the flesh and temptations, and
- It means starting brand new, believing in Christ, and accepting Him as your Saviour.

It's essential that you understand how Jesus died and was raised from the dead to atone for all our sins. Jesus gave us what we needed when he died on the cross. He shed his blood for every sin and curse. He defeated evil. And through his blood, we are saved and our sins forgiven. We are washed clean.

Jesus said, in Corinthians 6:19-20:

"Do you know that your bodies are the temples of the Holy Spirit, who is in you, whom you have received from God? You are not your own; you were bought at a price. Therefore, honour God with your bodies."

Over the years, many people have asked me to explain my understanding of the Holy Spirit and the Spirit's anointing. What does the Holy Spirit do? The Holy Spirit is allowed to communicate with us, if permitted by God—I don't invoke or conjure the Spirit, it happens spontaneously as it's only one way. I hear the message the Spirit brings to me.

There are also times when I see black spots that I believe are demonic entities. When I do God's work, as I'm doing right now, writing this book, I'm being watched. For those times, I light a candle and pray.

Once you begin developing your gifts, the impressions you receive become more sensitive, and you will become more aware of what is around you, both externally and internally. You learn how to distinguish and process what is going on within your physical, emotional, and mental body. Various techniques, such as creative visualization, affirmations, colours, and sounds, also help you learn how to let go and heal your mind, body, and spirit. You are responsible for working from the heart.

The third eye is your connection to the spiritual world, and I have taught various visualization techniques to help stimulate it. Its purpose is to help you tune into your surroundings using your five senses, but I prefer to work with one sense at a time. Since we store everything we've experienced in this lifetime within our cellular memory, a simple way to heal is through touch, colour, and sound.

My primary goal has always been to connect with another person's soul, which is why I decided to become a Reiki master, allowing me to work with the energy fields surrounding the human body. This type of spiritual healing has always existed and is the simplest form of it. Jesus talks about healing with his hands in the Bible. You invoke the Spirit from the highest point of unconditional love in the heart, and pray from a distance through visualization.

When I think about the way healing takes place, it's really about one energy meeting another. It's a union where two souls meet, much like the spiritual readings I provide. When this union of souls takes place, it's always the most beautiful and exciting experience because it's always unique. Healing takes initiative.

To all the healers out there and any in the making, no matter what path you go down, when you choose to be an instrument of healing and your intentions come from a loving heart, you're invoking the highest power—love. It can take on a life of its own.

Where man's limit ends, God's work does not. What do I mean by this? What we learn on this Earth as human beings limits our knowledge and beliefs. We look for scientific proof or explanations for everything. God is beyond our capacity to understand from a human perspective. He is above science, above explanations. He is infinite and limitless. Anything is possible with Him.

Chapter 16

Evil

Evil is not just a state of consciousness. It has origin, energy, and intent, unlike God who unites, evil works to divide. For lightworkers, that division is personal—dark forces follow you, trying to disrupt your mission and silence your purpose. They prey on the mind, injecting disturbing thoughts and horrific images, weakening our spiritual defences and using those closest to us—sometimes even in dreams—to access our hearts.

Seeing the Darkness

What does evil look like to someone like me?

I often see it in the form of black orbs, like flies hovering in a space, or dark dots circling people and homes. Sometimes, it appears as a black vortex—dense and magnetic—formed by others' negative thoughts. I've seen shadows take human form. I've even smelled sulphur. These manifestations are the energetic footprints of malevolent forces.

Evil spirits use fear and guilt to torment us. Their strategy is psychological oppression disguised as our voice. That's why love is so powerful. Love cuts through the fog, breaks the illusion, and invites the light. When we live from the heart, we disarm darkness. Love brings healing. It allows us to forgive, to soften, and to reconnect with what's real and eternal.

When we come from a place of pureness, we can heal. When you let love into your heart and separate yourself from your overthinking mind, you can forgive. When I am confused, in crisis, or can't explain things, I turn to the scriptures for guidance. The anointing of the Spirit reveals the truth about

God in his word on issues within the scriptures. I always say, don't worry, because today will take care of itself.

The negative experiences and trauma I lived through kept me locked in fear, and when you live in fear and allow yourself to break down, you are no longer engaged in life. You may have built a defence mechanism to protect you, but does all that emotional trauma keep you in the dark? It kept me from being confident and moving forward. That all changed when the Spirit anointed me.

Fear and Programming

We must break free from our programming to think, feel, and believe in a way that is truly our own. For a long time, I allowed my emotional trauma to create an element of fear within me. Overcoming this fear paved the way for forgiveness and gave me the space to heal and work through my issues. That doesn't mean I've worked out all of my problems, nor does it mean I'm now perfect. It doesn't mean I have all the answers. However, I see the good that comes out of it, whether in my life or other people's lives.

Society programs us from birth and instills fear in us from a very young age. Many times, religion is behind our fears. I realized that being raised Catholic created many fears in me, and I feel I was the culprit behind some of my self-sabotage. From my experience and understanding it has to do with the evil one: Satan.

Satan wants to destroy our spirit. His ultimate victory is to destroy God's precious servants and the lightworkers on Earth. He will try anything and everything to break you down and bring you into darkness, away from God's love and mercy. The devil entices people with sex, drugs, secret societies, and addictions. He lures you away from anything godly and tries to provide secret knowledge dealing with the occult. Everything that dishonours God and honours Satan is how the devil lures you away.

Evil spirits can come into your home at a time when you are at your most vulnerable. Satan lures you in. He preys on you through rejection, abandonment, and sexual addiction—anything to break you down psychologically and make you feel like you're all alone in this world. He will make you question, "Where is God in this situation?" He will make you feel like God has abandoned you in your moment of need.

The devil's sole mission is to destroy God's worshippers, and they tend to be the ones at the most risk. Like there is a hierarchy of God's angels, there is also a hierarchy in Satan's kingdom. Don't forget, Satan was cast out of Heaven as he was responsible for the first sin ever: pride. With him, a third of the angels were cast out of Heaven too. Because Satan knew how God ran his kingdom, he tried to replicate the same structure in his kingdom of evil.

Curses and Generational Chains

Evil can take many forms, and one of the most misunderstood is the curse. Sometimes it's born of jealousy or spite, when someone wishes to harm another out of pure malice. You may not believe in such things, but I've witnessed them. There are generational curses, passed on like poison through a bloodline. I've seen it happen when someone harbours so much hate or rage toward another that they curse not only the person, but also their descendants. That kind of energy, when left unchecked, becomes a pattern of bad luck or tragic circumstances, repeating itself from parent to child, and again to a grandchild.

I won't spend too much time on this now—there will be a future book dealing with that—but I need you to understand the breadth of evil. It's not always dramatic. Sometimes it's quiet. A whisper. A pattern. A bruise passed down in silence.

The Day I Spoke My Truth

In my 40s, I had to face something I'd been avoiding my entire life: my father. One day, without warning, he looked at me and said with a chilling detachment, "Look at what I created."

The words hit hard, but then I had a vision. It was my grandmother, his mother. She appeared clearly and calmly said, "Now is your opportunity to speak your truth."

So I did.

I gathered all my courage and asked, "How can you look at me like that—as if I'm nothing? As if I'm just your mistake. You've never truly seen me. All you see is your shame. But I'm not a mistake. I'm a beautiful, loving person. And from this moment forward, I'm giving you the chance to know me for who I truly am."

He started to cry.

That was the beginning of something new. Not just for me—for both of us. Because when you speak the truth, even when it's hard, something shifts. Darkness loses ground. Light rushes in.

The Rage That Follows

My husband, Steve, has struggled with a spirit of rage since he was a little boy. His biological father abandoned his mother before he was even born. That wound—abandonment from the womb—is something we both share. It was one of the first things that brought us together.

His mother got married when Steve was still an infant, and later had a daughter with her new husband. But his childhood was not peaceful. His stepsister tormented him constantly, manipulating situations to her advantage, weaponizing her father's blind devotion. When things didn't go her way, she'd make sure Steve got in trouble. It was control disguised as love. The rage that built inside him followed him into adulthood—until we brought it into the light.

One evening, Steve lovingly prepared a beautiful family dinner. But as we sat down to eat, we realized Mathew wasn't at the table. Steve called out, gently at first, then louder. No response.

The frustration began. I could feel it rising, not just because Mathew was being disrespectful, but also because Steve had worked hard to provide a moment of family connection.

Meanwhile, Mathew was upstairs, immersed in a video game, totally unaware of the energy building downstairs. I watched it unfold and knew what was happening. I heard it clearly in my spirit: *Be careful. This demon is going to try to use your son to create anger within your husband.*

Then came the trigger.

Mathew shouted back, "You made me lose my game!"

Steve exploded, "You're so unappreciative! I bought these expensive pieces of fish for you!"

But in that moment, I stepped in. I turned to Steve and said, "Do you not realize I see spirits? I know the ones that come from God—and the ones that don't."

That shifted the atmosphere. Just enough.

What people don't understand is that the devil is busy, especially with our children. Devices and games are more than distractions. They are spiritual traps. We are losing our family dynamic because of the division these things create. And when children are spiritually disconnected, the enemy finds its way in.

I'd seen it coming. That morning, I noticed the dark energy around Steve. It wasn't the first time. It shows up most clearly when he's tired, short on patience. Initially, I kept those observations to myself. But over time, as I grew spiritually, I began to speak up.

That morning, I warned him. I saw it. And later, it flared.

People often excuse these outbursts as "just being tired" or "stressed." But spiritual attacks can look exactly like that. Anger, jealousy, and revenge—these are not just emotions. They are doors. And it only takes a second of lowered consciousness for something dark to slip in and destroy everything.

Addiction and the Spirits That Linger

I know this truth intimately. I've lived it.

My addictions weren't just bad habits. They were emotional diseases—wounds in disguise. Through Gamblers Anonymous and the 12-step program, I learned what it means to surrender, to realize that alone we are powerless.

My addiction didn't start from nowhere. When I was a child, my father would take me to bars while my mother went off to play Bingo. I'd sit there and watch him gamble and play cards. I didn't stand a chance.

Some spirits stay earthbound. They've never fully crossed over. They cling to humans, attaching themselves to our lives so they can continue to experience what they crave: alcohol, sex, drugs, and control. When science and logic fall short, and there's no other explanation for the behaviour you're witnessing, know that 99.9% of the time, it's spiritual.

Breaking the Pattern

So many of my clients come to me saying the same thing, "I don't know why, but bad luck follows my family." And more often than not, I discover a generational curse—one rooted in jealousy or hatred, cast years ago but still taking root in the lives of the innocent.

Evil is strategic. It disguises itself as a coincidence. But behind the scenes it is creating confusion, chaos, and division—anything to keep you from evolving into a higher being.

Some dark forces even masquerade as lightworkers, using spiritual language to mislead and distract. That's why we must 'test the spirit.' The Word of God is not just a book—it's a sword. A compass. A line in the sand.

As it says in Luke 10:18 20:

> "And he said unto them, I beheld Satan as lightning fall from Heaven. I give unto you power to tread on serpents and scorpions, and over all the power of the enemy: and nothing shall by any means hurt you… but rather rejoice, because your names are written in Heaven."

Yes, evil spirits exist. Yes, they torment and oppress. There are levels to this, and I will go deeper into those levels in a future book.

But this book? This one is about awakening.

It's about what becomes possible when you open your heart to Jesus Christ, and you stop running. When you trust your spirit to our heavenly Father and start seeing the world—and yourself—through the lens of truth.

Because evil is real.

But so is your power.

And the light always wins.

Chapter 17

Communicating With The Spirit World

Before I fully understood or accepted my gift of connecting with those who had passed, my mother-in-law, Diane, often spoke of her mother and how deeply she loved her. Her mother had died at 55 when Diane was in her thirties. Sometimes I'd ask questions; other times Diane would share small memories. But I had never seen a photo of her.

One evening, I dreamt of a woman who introduced herself as Lillian LeBlanc—Steve's grandmother. She looked to be in her thirties, dressed in a grey tweed jacket and skirt, her hair twisted into a bun. In the dream, she gently took my hand and held it.

It left me unsettled—it felt too real to dismiss The next morning, I told my mother-in-law.

"Guess who I dreamt about? Your mother!"

I described the woman exactly. Diane went straight to her room and returned with a photo from Steve's baptism. My breath caught. There she was—same outfit, same hairstyle. The woman in the dream was a real person.

Recognizing the Gift

Though shaken, I still closed off that part of myself. I didn't know how to place these dreams. Were they imagination? Was there meaning? I had no framework, just the lingering feeling that something was reaching across. Time and again, I resisted the truth of my gift.

My paternal grandmother, Prudenza, had come from Italy to meet us when I was eleven years old. She had saved for nearly 20 years just to spend time with her grandchildren in Canada. I only had a week with her, but I felt so loved—even across a language barrier. She passed away the following year.

At a cousin's wedding years later, I met my aunt Leonilda for the first time.

"So you're the Yolanda she always talked about," she said with tears. "She said you were special. Over and over."

Those words haunted me. In that short amount of time, my grandmother must have felt and known I had a special gift. I often feel her presence. Special. Gifted. But I didn't feel that way. I pushed it down, tried to be normal. Tried to be logical. But I often felt her presence.

When I feel sad, she comes to visit. I feel a tickling, tingling sensation and warmth in my body, or she'll play with my hair to comfort me. Every spirit has a different vibration, and you can feel different sensations every time it touches you. For example, when Lyn visits, she lets me know by touching my left arm. A male spirit will generally touch your dominant hand, and a female spirit your other one. I gave a spiritual reading to my friend, Maria, many years ago. She is also sensitive, meaning she can sense things. When I'm feeling down, Maria will call me out of the blue and say, "I feel your grandmother, she doesn't want you to be sad." Our loved ones speak in whispers—quiet signs, sudden memories, unexpected warmth.

I once read in a spiritual book that if our grandmothers have passed away before we were born, they can become our angels and guides.

My maternal grandmother, Melina, has always been by my side. Especially in moments when I feel exhausted or ready to give up, she finds a way to show me she's near. Our first encounter happened in my twenties, shortly after I gave birth to my first son, during what I now recognize as the beginning of my spiritual awakening.

That weekend, my Aunt Anna Marie, a gifted musician, had gathered us at my mother's house for an evening of music. We were all jamming in the living room when my mother began to feel unwell. Concerned, we took her to the emergency room. Tests revealed her white blood cell count was unusually high.

While we waited, my mother began to sing *The House of the Rising Sun*. As she stood and sang, I saw a spiritual presence appear beside her: a woman in a yellow and brown dress adorned with birds and flowers, her salt-and-pepper hair cascading around a face marked by a distinctive mole.

After the song, I shared what I saw. My family stared at me, stunned. They said I had just described my grandmother on the day she was buried. The dress was the same. The mole, unmistakable! Yet I had never met her, never seen photos, never attended the funeral. It was my first clear spiritual encounter with Grandma Melina. I believe she came to reassure me that my mother would be okay.

Then Came the Fire Alarm: When the Spirits Speak

It was 2019. Uncle Gary had just visited. We spent the afternoon reminiscing—warm conversation, shared laughter, a soft goodbye. He mentioned not feeling well. A few weeks later, my fire alarm went off for no reason. No smoke. No fire. I checked every room, even knocked on the neighbour's door—nothing.

I assumed it was defective, so I returned it to the Home Depot store where I bought it. It shrieked the entire car ride and kept wailing in the store! The customer service representative joked that something had possessed it. I exchanged it for a new one and tried to move on.

Three days later, the call came—Uncle Gary had passed.

Only then did it click: it wasn't a faulty alarm. It was my grandmother, Melina, trying to get my attention. And I hadn't been listening. I installed the new alarm. Not long after, it started ringing again. This time, I listened.

I got another call—my mother had been rushed to the hospital. That day marked the beginning of her dementia diagnosis. That was the moment I truly woke up. The signs had always been there. I just hadn't learned how to hear them. Now I know—when change is near, my grandmother comes.

How did all this fit into my life? Where was I going with all this? The answers came when I understood that nothing happens by accident.

God is always at work. He patiently prunes us so that we can grow in strength through pain and suffering, understanding His teachings and how to transform our lives through our relationship with Him and ourselves.

Yolanda Tarantino

"Jesus, knowing their thoughts, took a little child and had him stand beside him. Then he said to them, whoever welcomes this little child welcomes me, and whoever welcomes me welcomes my father. To enter the kingdom of Heaven, you must become like a child, for children are pure of heart."

(Luke 9:47)

Chapter 18

Spiritual Readings, Healings, and Cleansings

When I first began offering readings, I did so from the comfort of my home. Eventually, I started sharing them at Psychic Expos and the Spiritual Healing Church. I provided these readings voluntarily, sharing clairvoyant insights, prophetic words, and messages of hope and healing. The fire of the Holy Spirit stirred something deep within me, leading me to my true calling. That's when I became a minister, devoted to serving others.

Over the past 20 years, I have conducted numerous spiritual readings and have learned to identify the pain that many of my clients have endured. They usually come to me with similar types of emotional trauma that I have experienced, especially sexual abuse and issues inflicted on them from loved ones who have passed.

How can I help set them free from the pain and suffering inflicted upon them as innocent souls? I need to let them know they are not alone. I have to be able to listen even though I may not always have an answer, and understand that at times, silence is the best remedy. I need to be present and let those coming to me for help and guidance know that because they've come this far, they can go a little further and get the professional help they need. I want to help give people closure so they can heal. Whenever I receive messages I tend to see spiritual bodies, ghosts, spiritual beings, and guides. These spirits appear to me in a form that will allow me to know who they are.

An Indian chief will appear to me as an Indian chief. Other times, I see symbols. If I am sitting with someone and a vision of a feather appears, my Spirit guides are trying to indicate that this person is a shaman or one in the process of becoming one. When I see or feel departed loved ones, it varies depending on the spirit's evolution whether they have enough light in them, or have risen high enough in frequency. It's all about vibration and frequency. Sometimes a departed one will give me a sign of their illness. I will notice a body part that does not appear healthy, such as an unhealthy intestine. Sometimes I feel the actual incident of the sickness or how they have passed.

Before I understood my gift, I would constantly go to the hospital because I thought I was sick or there was something physically wrong with me. It didn't make sense at the time because I would be standing in front of someone, and I would get a shooting pain on the right side of my temple. I genuinely thought there was something wrong with my body. In reality, it was their loved one showing me, allowing me to feel their brain aneurysm.

I have learned that when you see a black spot in one of the chakras, it can sometimes mean there is a health problem manifesting itself in that person. For example, I have done a reading for someone where I noticed a significant amount of negative energy surrounding their liver. Usually my guides are doctors and healers who can tell me the root cause. When it deals with the liver, it is generally surrounding anger, possibly from trauma, which has blocked and trapped their energy. And over time it becomes stagnant.

What I am doing is not a cure; I am simply raising awareness about the issue for them. My clients then have the free will to decide if they want to stay with that awareness or do the work to change it.

In the etheric body, disease can stay there and sit and wait for a couple of years before moving into the physical body. To stop it from manifesting in the physical body, the required work is needed to heal from within first, and release the stagnant energy that stops the flow in the body.

The goal is to utilize all available modalities to support your healing. That includes prayer, meditation, yoga, and consulting doctors, psychologists, or psychiatrists, among others. God and the Spirit can guide us, but we still need to utilize all available resources to achieve the necessary healing of our mind, body, and spirit.

There are no rules as to what will work the best for you. Sometimes, departed ones leave me with imprints. They show me a specific sign or symbol that only the person in front of me will understand. For example, I did a reading for a man where all the spirit showed me was a single rose. I didn't realize what the rose meant. All I can do is interpret. When I told the man of my vision, he started to cry. Rose was the name of the little girl he had lost. He was astonished that I, knowing nothing about him, revealed something that helped him understand the message the spirit was trying to convey.

I have learned how to identify and associate symbols with what happens next. I have also found other clairvoyants who work in the healing profession, as well as others, like myself, who have developed and refined their healing gifts. The beauty of my work lies in witnessing the transformation in people. Sometimes it happens in an instant, while at other times it can take years to develop. I work with professional healers whom I recommend to my clients. God has placed wonderful people on my path. There is room in the universe for everyone. In one of my sessions, a woman who came to see me had lost her 29-year-old daughter, leaving behind three children. Her daughter had been in a relationship with an abusive boyfriend who kept her isolated and forced her to stop speaking with her parents. After she passed, her mother had survivor's guilt. In one of my visions, a young woman kept showing me a tattoo with wings. When I described to the woman what I was seeing, she told me about the tattoo she wanted to get to honour her daughter, and her sister also wanted to get a tattoo with angel wings. My reading gave her the confirmation she needed that she could communicate with her daughter. The relief on her face was palpable.

As a lightworker, I can sense or pick up on emotional blockages that result from trauma, mainly because they show up repeatedly during readings. The more times it pops up, the more stagnant it is in someone's energy. Whenever you think or feel negatively towards someone, it can manifest itself within your body and keep you in a stale or stuck state. In these situations, you are not tapping into the best of energies.

There is a direct correlation between holding grievances in your heart and disease. When you hang on to these feelings and thoughts and don't practice forgiveness, it can develop further in your physical body. We all need to forgive the people who have harmed or hurt us. We need to repent for our sins because we are all human and because we have a physical existence.

When we don't take responsibility for our actions, our body manifests physical signs such as pain or illness. When we hold on to anger, jealousy, feelings of unworthiness, or become rebellious, we can also develop addictions. Whenever we experience all of these emotions, there is an area of our life that is demonized or oppressed. In this state, we are more vulnerable to these evil forces. We must realize that there is a constant battle between mind, body, and spirit to fight off these entities.

At times, I am fortunate enough to know women who have become empowered and walked away from volatile relationships, something I couldn't help do for my mother. When these women understand that they are loved unconditionally by our heavenly Father, a light bulb turns on, and a new beginning dawns within them. I want to awaken the spirit within each of you as it awakened within me. There is more to this life than being born and dying, more than just existing and being in constant chaos. We need to sit quietly to hear God's audible voice within us.

God provides these experiences as a test; a learning experience meant to help us grow and evolve so we can strive towards God's perfection, also known as "grace" or "virtue."

Remaining stuck blocks our relationship with God. We tend to look outside ourselves to find our identity and understand what the truth is when we should be looking within, where God is. We tend to fill ourselves up with personas and false programming of what we think we need. The soul chooses the life lessons it needs to experience on Earth. Your soul chooses the mother whose womb it will enter ,and selects the obstacles it wants to learn from and experience in this life.

In addition to spiritual readings, I also cleanse homes of certain types of energy. People come to me because they feel strange vibrations in their home, like something is off. They feel a sense of dread or panic. Somctimes they feel the hair on their arms stand up, but nothing is visible, typically indicating the presence of negative energy or spirits in the home.

Negative energies in the home can affect your mood, your sleep, and your anxiety. They can create a sense of fear in children. Children may be afraid to go to bed at night. When we let people into our homes, we also allow them to bring their energy, which can be either positive or negative. Always be cautious of who you let into your house.

"When an unclean spirit goes out of a man, he goes through dry places, seeking rest; and finding none, he says, 'I will return to my house from which I came.' And when he comes, he finds it swept and put in order. Then he goes and takes with him seven other spirits more wicked than himself, and they enter and dwell there; and the last state of that man is worse than the first."

(Luke 11:24-26)

Yolanda Tarantino

Chapter 19

Spirituality Versus Religion

My struggle comes more from the conflict in my mind regarding religion. There is a big difference between being religious and being spiritual. Although religion has its place in this world, I've come to realize that worshipping the Lord in Spirit and having a spiritual relationship with Him is more than just following religious rules and instructions.

People must understand true spirituality. I believe in the word of God, but it does not stop me from being a spiritual person. Religion refers to a set of organized beliefs and practices shared by a community or group of people, whereas spirituality is more of an individual practice. Spirituality is more about cultivating a sense of peace and purpose within oneself. I can't stress enough how important it is for me to speak about spirituality. Reading the Bible provides me with the spiritual nourishment I need to understand the complexities of life.

As it is written in John 4:1: *"Dear friends, do not believe in every Spirit, but test the Spirit to see if the Spirit is from God, as there are many false prophets that have gone out in the world."*

Attending church every Sunday may make you religious, but it does not necessarily make you spiritual. I believe spirituality is about having a connection with God, living by His word, and spreading His message of love. Whenever I have supernatural experiences, the Lord renews my faith in Him.

When I speak about having a relationship with the Lord, it's about worshipping God with all the love in your heart. It's about being with Christ and speaking the word of God, and it is through this union that we worship in the spirit. Having the emotion and the heart to say the words out loud and witness the power in the name of Jesus, helps defend us from the wickedness of the devil.

I have attended a few spiritual services where people who have received anointings with the Holy Spirit share messages with the congregation. On one occasion, I was praying to Archangel Michael for protection. At that moment, the pastor came up to me and said I can see Archangel Michael with you. He was protecting me. That is something that is also very important to me, the power of prayer and invoking the Spirit of God. Since we store everything we've lived through in this lifetime within our cellular memory, a simple way to heal is through touch, colour, and sound.

When we look at Jesus, the Son of God, sent to us in the form of a human being, He is a great healer. There are countless testimonials in the New Testament of His innumerable miracles and healings. He healed people with cerebral palsy and epilepsy, as well as delivered individuals from evil spirits.

Every time I think of Jesus and the healing He performed, I think of the inspirational song, "He Healeth Me." When we call out to Jesus and ask Him to work in and through us, He lifts us. God never gives us more than we can handle. He works in such subtle ways, with small revelations, much like peeling away the layers of an onion. We can all learn the personal truth of who we are as a child of Christ.

In John 14:17, Jesus speaks about the Spirit who reveals the truth about God: the Holy Spirit. John 14:26 also talks about a guide who, if we believe in them, will send us the Spirit of Truth. The Spirit of Truth teaches us all we need to know about God and the Kingdom to come. We have the opportunity to work it out in this lifetime, allowing us to heal, grow, and gain inner understanding. Being saved by Jesus through an encounter with Him made a greater difference and had a more profound impact.

The Bible has been my go-to book for any question that I need answers for. It serves as a daily guide to help us navigate our lives here on Earth. I have found every answer through prayer and meditation. These tools allow me to focus, stay present, and bring me great joy, as well as a deeper love for God. The Bible helps me to know Him more intimately.

If you study the New Testament, it is full of logic and common sense. The Bible is very straightforward. It spiritually fulfills my needs. It taught me that love is the ultimate tool against the evil spiritual forces that are constantly at work.

Not only that, but the Bible teaches us how to worship and pray. How to be a better human being and become a child of Christ. It can give us hope and peace, and help us work towards an everlasting life. There is a reference Jesus makes in the New Testament, Matthew 6:22-23:

> *"The lamp of the body is the eye. If therefore your eye is good, your whole body will be full of light. But if your eye is bad, your whole body will be full of darkness. If therefore the light that is in you is darkness, how great is that darkness!"*

Bottom line, I'm still healing, and I know God is working within and through me to fine-tune me like a precious instrument. As a result, I can feel great highs and lows. Whenever I feel low, I sit and meditate. Then the Holy Spirit falls upon me and I'll cry tears of joy. I've had a few addictions in my life, such as food, gambling, and smoking. Those addictions kept me from God by keeping me emotionally numb.

When I came to Christ, I felt the anointing of the Holy Spirit that Jesus speaks about in the New Testament. If we come to Christ and love with our hearts and minds, it is a gift no one will lose.

Healing is the power to love unconditionally, much like the heavenly Father and his son's love for us. Your spirit is the ultimate healer, and we can continually heal ourselves through the power of unconditional love. The core message on our journey of enlightenment is that the power of love heals us from the inside out. When you embody the power of love, your body can continually rejuvenate itself.

At one of my church services, I spoke about the Holy Spirit. When you read the words in the Bible, you can put the inspired word of God in your heart and implement it moving forward. Furthermore, if we choose to forgive others, it is the ultimate weapon against the rulers of darkness, and in that moment we are set free. Once we allow forgiveness to take hold, we will know our truth built on faith. We learn to trust, and we can have peace of mind.

The Bible is the word of God, which is the sword of the Spirit. When you start speaking the word of God around those who are not with God, it stirs them, and you can see the rebellion in them come out. It riles up the devil the most. He hates anything that reminds him of the true God, as he is the one who seeks idolization like a true God.

It's easier for people to believe that God does not exist and that there is no supernatural war waging, and to lead a life blinded by all the Devil's distractions. Indifference. Ignorance. Denial. It has been going on since the first rebellion when Lucifer (the morning star or "light-bringer") was kicked out of Heaven. Lucifer convinced other angels to turn on God, to turn away from God, all because he wanted to be worshipped.

> *"How you have fallen from heaven,*
> *morning star, son of the dawn!*
> *You have been cast down to the earth,*
> *you who once laid low the nations!*
> *You said in your heart,*
> *"I will ascend to the heavens;*
> *I will raise my throne*
> *above the stars of God;*
> *I will sit enthroned on the mount of assembly,*
> *on the utmost heights of Mount Zaphon.*
> *I will ascend above the tops of the clouds;*
> *I will make myself like the Most High."*
> *But you are brought down to the realm of the dead,*
> *to the depths of the pit."*

(Isaiah 14:12-15)

How can we prepare ourselves amid the business of life? How can we see God at work in our lives? How does God manifest himself in our everyday lives when we are in pain and suffering?

The mind always brings in some type of memory or half-truth to counteract this. It's happened to me often, blocking and derailing me from my true path. Many times along my journey to discovering God, I would hear a little negative voice in the back of my head trying to dissuade me from the righteous path to God.

When this happens, you need to squash it immediately because it is making you doubt yourself, just like I doubted myself. You doubt God.

Whenever this happens, we need to ask ourselves:

Where is this coming from?

Is it coming from our ego?

Is it coming from how you are programmed and the belief system you learned?

Is it trying to suppress you from thinking freely and being open-minded to other planes of existence that do not fit into any logical explanation?

These are all questions that went through my mind as I analyzed things to uncover the truth.

You must be vigilant at every moment. You need to always look at your life and ask yourself: here am I in my life with my relationship with God, as I should know Him? And you need to remind yourself constantly: God loves me and I want to love Him unconditionally in return. I want to hear God's voice, and I want him to be the architect of my life.

Do not settle for half-truths.

When you are living your truth in union with the Spirit, any half-truths can create illusions that will bring in self-doubt. When you live in God and have the Spirit of God within you, you are set free and at peace. God shines His truth upon you. He will lead you on a journey of self-discovery, which will bring you to a spiritual revelation, one of the most beautiful things I have witnessed through meditation and prayer—a powerful union with God and myself through His beautiful Son, Jesus Christ, the highest form of existence and living on the Earth plane.

I once had a client, a true non-believer, who would constantly test everything to find something wrong so he could justify his disbelief. One day I said to him, "For those who believe, an explanation is not necessary, but for those who do not believe, no explanation is possible."

In that pain, we tend to hurt ourselves with addictions, self-sabotage, self-hate, and others around us. One example is when you see a happy person. They are coming from the purest place of all—LOVE—which is the ultimate weapon. And it's essential to stay connected constantly.

When we know that God the Father and His Son love us, He reveals the Holy Spirit, leaving no room for doubt. We cannot do anything on our own. If we stay connected to God, we receive all of God's blessings. But first, we have to get right with God. We must be honest, as He wants us to be true to Him.

In John 15:7: *"If you abide in me and my words abide in you, you can ask for anything you want and you will receive it."*

How do we learn to hear God's voice? We have to become quiet inside.

As I mentioned previously in the Gospel of John, God refers to pruning the vine, a metaphor that explains how He is preparing us. But what is God preparing us for? He wants us to be His messengers on Earth. He wants us to bring others to His bountiful love. He wants the people around us to see how God's warriors ask for something with unwavering faith and receive it. We are all given gifts and strengths, but we need to learn to tap into them. We need to learn how to turn our misfortune into an opportunity for good.

You may have heard a saying, "Life doesn't happen to us, it happens for us."

We need to be able to take a bad situation or a negative experience and figure out the lesson. Use these opportunities as a chance for growth.

I believe God is within us, regardless of our faith, and we need to remain connected to Him. While writing this book, I received a message from Jesus. I saw an image of Saint Faustina and another of Jesus and His Divine Mercy. Jesus was showing me at this present age that most of the healing comes from the two rays coming out from his heart.

When we start on a journey of self-discovery, we become renewed as Jesus heals all our ills and ailments. Through God, He releases and teaches us what we need to do to heal within ourselves. He makes us self-aware. When we become conscious, we become open and can heal on a cellular level.

The message He is sending is the heart of mercy. He grants us the mercy for whatever situation we find ourselves in, whether it's:

· Forgiving all the people who have wronged us, or

· Confessing and taking responsibility for all the wrong we have done.

We are not perfect beings, having done or still doing things that are not exemplary. We have probably hidden these situations somewhere deep in our hearts because we don't want to think about them. But letting go of these things frees us to heal. These are some of the things you benefit from when you embark on your journey of spirituality. The most significant gift is receiving God's mercy.

Anyone can know God. Anyone can know Jesus. Anyone can have a personal relationship with them. We need only reach out and ask. Jesus didn't just come for the believers. Jesus came for those who needed him. If you knock on his door, He will open it. You don't have to be Christian to ask Jesus for help. God performed miracles with people from all walks of life, including Mary of Magdalene, who was a prostitute. He delivered demons from people's bodies. He spoke with and helped people without housing and those who were beggars. He devoted his time to caring for the sick and the afflicted. He chose the company of the outcast over the elite and the healthy.

We will have abundance and knowledge if we stay connected to God and live fruitful lives. He doesn't want us to have a horrible and miserable life; He wants us to be happy and joyful. But what does that mean? It means we make time for God. We meditate so that we can hear His voice and listen to what He is saying to us.

Chapter 20

Meditation and Prayer

What is the difference between meditation and prayer?

- Prayer brings us into union with God.
- Meditation allows us to be present with our heart and listen to its whispers.

Both can help you move towards forgiveness and letting go of anything you've been holding on to. Clinging to anything negative keeps you in disease. Anger and unforgiveness keep you full of hate and in darkness. You need to forgive and let go of the past. Jesus' ministry is all about setting us free by forgiving others, no matter how they wronged you. But it needs to be a forgiveness that comes from a place of unconditional love.

But what if you can't forgive someone?

When Jesus hung on the cross, he took everything onto himself. He took every single sin known to man to the cross, and by believing in him, we receive his grace and a clean slate. He allowed us to be reborn in the spirit.

I know how hard it is to forgive someone. Sometimes when we are so angry, hurt, and in so much pain, we're blinded by our emotions, intuition and a conscious awareness of God. We need to learn to discern between our egos and that of God. When you can't forgive someone, ask God or Jesus to be your intercessor. We can say to God, "Right now, I can't forgive this person, but I know you can. I give it up to you."

When I pray for people, I go into a spiritual union with God as I understand him. I once saw a big hand the size of a large painting outstretched and open in my vision. I understood it as the healing hand of God was laid upon me.

God's hand heals. And I need to trust in the process. I have had many people come back and tell me afterwards of their own miraculous stories. Let go and give it all to God or Jesus. And watch miracles unfold in your life.

To achieve forgiveness while surrendering your pain and suffering, prayer and meditation are essential. They help to place us in an altered state of union with God and align our mind, heart, and spirit with the highest vibration of all—the mind of the Lord). Prayer is like meditation; it is the same. One of the ways I meditate is by quieting my mind and focusing on the colours of the rainbow. I learned to let go of the numbing pain. By letting go, I allowed God to fill all those voids. Just like the passage in the Bible from Mathew 11:25-30:

> *"My work is light, give me your burdens, says God, and I shall shed my light upon you."*

There are opposing forces all around us—physical, mental, and supernatural. You can either stand down or rise above them. Do not allow yourself to remain stuck in your pain. Rise above it.

One of my favourite meditations, which I still use today, is visualization. It is one that I also teach to my students. Imagine you're in a beautiful green space. You are ONE with nature. Put your hands in the soil. What does it feel like?

Visualize a beautiful spring flower with its vibrant diversified colours of purple, red, green, magenta, and yellow.

Visualize planting the flower in the ground and watching it come to life.

Visualize its roots as they extend and attach themselves to the minerals of Mother Earth.

As you're planting this beautiful flower into the earth, you are not only planting from the place of love, you are also planting your ideas and your goals for what you want in this life.

All of the seeds I have planted have produced fruit.

I perform this meditation daily, or as needed.

Chapter 21

Dreams and Symbolism

Symbolism is the use of icons to represent ideas or qualities, often attributed to natural objects or animals. Whether in our waking state or our dream state, symbols are all around us. It is essential to be aware of these symbols and the messages they convey.

The cross is a very powerful symbol, and many people associate it with Christianity. However, it represents much more—that Jesus endured the ultimate human suffering for all of us. He loved us so much; He gave up his life so we could be spiritually free from the chains that bound us, including those from the opposing forces around us. Regardless of who hurt him during his crucifixion, he forgave them to save us. Would you forgive the person who killed you? Jesus did. He is the essence of forgiveness. We don't realize it but God works and speaks through us every day. He speaks to us through dreams, also known as prophetic dreams, using symbols that can take a lifetime to understand.

My first experience with these types of dreams happened when I was a teenager. It was 1984. During the week, I would get up early to go to school and get home around three o'clock in the afternoon, exhausted from my consistently broken sleep and unbearable living situation. I would usually take a nap before supper and most evenings after supper. On the weekends, I would work at the gas station or the pharmacy. When I wasn't working, I would sometimes babysit Mark, an 18-month-old toddler and the son of my mother's close friend.

During one of my naps, a face appeared in my dream. It was a skeleton wearing a hood that covered the majority of its face. The dream was too scary to share with anyone, so I kept the experience to myself. Five months later, little Mark died. They discovered he had been born with a hole in his heart that never closed, and without treatment it had grown too big and no one, not even the doctors, had ever been aware of it.

Once I became more conscious of my gifts, I was able to look back and realize that I had seen the angel of death, but didn't understand the symbolism of the vision at the time. I have seen this angel many times throughout my lifetime since then, and it always saddens me when I do because it symbolizes someone's passing. I never know who will pass, but I know someone will. Even if it is shown who will pass, I am not allowed to vocalize it. I cannot interfere with God's plan. I am simply an instrument of God, to do His will as He instructs.

In most cases, I typically experience these types of prophetic dreams between 5 and 7 a.m.

One night, I dreamt of being in the clouds; I was standing on a crystal floor. The dream was so vivid and clear. Surrounding me were varying shades of purple—it was so beautiful. But when I looked down I saw a pit full of black snakes, thousands and thousands of them all writhing and wriggling. Although the snakes were trying to get to me, I felt safe and protected.

I came to understand that the snakes represented negative energies or evil spirits. There are many negative and evil energies and spirits, but God was protecting me. Remember, God speaks to us through dreams and symbols. He always has our backs.

If God is for you, who can be against you? As written in Luke 10:19:

"I have given you authority to trample on snakes and scorpions and to destroy all the enemy's power, and nothing will ever hurt you."

When I became a level three Reiki master, I had a vision of the kundalini serpent (the caduceus) climbing a rod, which is the universal symbol associated with medicine. I was thinking about someone who needed healing. Seeing that symbol helped me understand the energy we have within ourselves. We are spiritual beings, and Reiki is a tool that enables us to connect with our spiritual aspect.

Usually, when you see a serpent, your mind automatically associates it negatively. Symbols are powerful and conscious. Part of my spiritual awakening was learning how to break the cycle of our earthly programming and go beyond what we believe. I understood that my awakening was profound and tied to the gift of healing God had given me. I realized that the emblem of the serpent, rod, and angel wings represented healing.

One evening, I was meditating in my living room, working with different chakras and energies. I was concentrating on my third eye when I saw a window illuminated with beautiful golden light. In the centre, I saw a magnificent six-pointed star. It was white and silvery tinged with blue, similar to the Star of David. It was beyond gorgeous. I also saw a chalice and having studied some symbolism, knew it represented the Cup of Knowledge. I also saw a lovely rose, which made me think of Mother Mary. Golden rectangular shapes surrounded me on the wall where a portal was open. There, I saw a silhouette of my spiritual body, identical to what I look like, but illuminated in iridescent gold. I saw my spiritual profile and I realized I could leave my body to travel across different levels of the spiritual world, known as 'astral projection,' even in a waking state.

Visions through meditation revealed to me the potential and what the outcome would be like. Like the flame of the Olympic torch, I would pass on the flame. I learned to conquer my fears by feeling my experiences through meditation and some of the spiritual classes I taught. The more I paid attention to the symbols in this world, the more I became familiar with how God was trying to communicate with me. In time, you can do the same.

Yolanda Tarantino

Conclusion

I am a seeker of the truth. I have changed my entire life and my perspective on the spirit of God within. It's like turning on a switch which allows you to break away from the negativity of the mind and the things of this world that keep you imprisoned. Set yourself free and learn the ways of the spirit of God and be forever transformed in mind, body, and spirit.

I leave you with two final thoughts.

First, I encourage everyone to read the Bible and discover the truth for themselves. The Bible is a book that has been used for over two thousand years, written by people inspired by a man who sacrificed himself for us.

Prayer and meditation are powerful tools as they invoke the Spirit of God. Listen intuitively to the small voice within as well as through meditation and prayer. It is also important to have a strong union with God. When I say union or marriage with God, I'm referring to worshipping God with all the love in your heart. Embody the mind of Christ to be able to speak the word of God. Have the emotion and the heart to speak the words of God out loud. There is power in the name Jesus Christ and that is the union God gives, allowing us to worship in the spirit.

Second, have a child-like heart.

The disciples came to Jesus and asked, in Matthew 18:1-5: *"Who, then, is the greatest in the Kingdom of Heaven?"* He called a little child to him and placed the child in their midst. And he said: *"Truly I tell you, unless you change and become like little children, you will never enter the kingdom of Heaven. Therefore, whoever takes the lowly position of this child is the greatest in the Kingdom of Heaven. And whoever welcomes one such child in my name welcomes me."*

"Truly I tell you, anyone who will not receive the Kingdom of God like a little child will never enter it." (Luke 18:17)

The importance of this message is that we need to unlearn everything, more specifically, the way we were programmed. We need only to come into our spiritual selves.

We must become like children, with completely open minds and hearts, to understand the Kingdom of Heaven. We can't do this if we go there with predetermined ideas and thoughts of what we think we might know. We need to be open and receptive like a child who goes willingly and trustingly to the Lord, which is why I named my first book *Awakening the Spirit Within*. I wanted to share that you can have a spiritual and supernatural relationship with God and live within His spirit.

One teaching Jesus emphasized is: LOVE ONE ANOTHER.

Love heals all. Love brings rejuvenation, light, joy, and lasting peace that is open to every soul.

I urge you to live—LIVE IN CHRIST!

The truth I have shared inspires you to examine your own life and awaken the spirit within.

Testimonials

"Yolanda has known our family for just a little over 10 years now. The first time I met with her, I had very minimal expectations of connecting with any of my loved ones because I never really believed that anyone had the ability to do that.

So why did I even meet with her in the first place if I was a non-believer?

A good friend of mine told me about her and assured me that she could help me connect with my deceased loved ones, in particular my father. I was very hesitant and reluctant; however, I took my friend's word, what's the absolute worst thing that could happen by seeing her? To be honest, I had already programmed myself to be disappointed and went to meet her with little to no hope.

When it was over, I was completely shocked and mind blown. She exceeded my every expectation when she shared experiences and specific details with me that no one would ever normally know. She shared memories and moments that I had with my brother-in-law, father and grandfather. I absolutely knew she wasn't making anything up because of the intimate details she shared. I truly felt chills during our session, and I could feel my father's presence while she spoke to me. Chills literally ran up my spine multiple times when I was with Yolanda. I knew that my loved ones were there with us. The lights flickered and danced when she spoke to me about them. When I finished my session with her, I felt love, warmth and joy, because I never in my life would have ever thought I could reconnect with anyone from my past.

Yolanda managed to put a smile on my mother's face, which was a difficult thing to do as she was grieving the loss of my father. She helped us all to deal with our emotions and taught us how to smile again when all we knew was a world of sadness and pain. Ever since that very first session over ten years ago, we haven't lost touch with her. We continue to call her every once in a while, although not as often as we'd like, because life gets hectic. However, when we do see her, we are excited for the entire week leading up to her visit. We usually do family sessions with her. Not only do we get to reconnect with the people we miss so dearly, but we get to connect and just chat with Yolanda, someone who is not only our medium, but someone who has become part of our family, a dear friend whom we trust with our secrets and someone who shines light when all we can see is darkness. God bless Yolanda. She is someone that everyone should see at least once in their lives. She not only offers her services, but also speaks words of knowledge and demonstrates what it is to believe, have faith and to live life in peace.

Thank you for becoming such an inspiring friend and someone we consider part of our family."

- *Lisa Mezzacappa.*

"**The first time I met Yolanda** was back in 2012 or 2013, around two years after my father passed. My friend's father had passed, and our mothers became friends through the ordeal. My mother informed me that Linda and her family had organized to meet with a woman named Yolanda. She apparently could communicate with spirits. I didn't hesitate one second. I wanted to be there. I wanted to talk to my father. I believe that some of us have gifts and are blessed with the ability to be an instrument through which spirits can communicate and reach out.

I was running late that night, I can't remember why, but by the time I arrived, I was almost an hour late. I rang the doorbell and as I stepped into the house, I could hear my mother tell her, that's my daughter. As I started to walk into the house, I heard Yolanda exclaim, "so that's who he's been waiting for." I knew immediately she was referring to my father. "Your father hasn't said anything until now; he was waiting for you to arrive." My heart stopped. I was somewhat shocked. They offered me a seat right beside her on her right. Funny, it's not until I am writing this that I am thinking about the Apostles Creed, a prayer in which it proclaims Jesus is seated on the right side of the Father. Not sure if that means anything, but it just popped into my head. As if someone put it there. Something I would later in life learn a lot about with Yolanda.

I had talked to my father leading up to the night. Yolanda encouraged us to speak to our loved ones in private when no one else was around, and I did so all the time, particularly before I met Yolanda. Asking him to provide answers to questions I had for him. I felt a lot of guilt for not being by my father's side when he took his last breath. I was with him until the night prior, and he passed that morning. My entire family was there, and I was at home. I felt bad for not rushing over or staying that night. I knew he would pass away, but I think I just could not bring myself to be there to see that. I knew because that night I felt very strong negative energy circling around my father. I had really bad chills and it was perfectly warm in my parent's home. I felt like these bad spirits wanted to grab at my father.

I remember going into my spare room where I kept the Virgin Mary, and I knelt at her feet and told her to let my father know that if he wanted to go that he didn't need to wait for me. I told my father to go be with God. As I rose from prayer the phone rang and my mother was crying. My father had just passed. I was so lost for two years until that very night. Until Yolanda came into my life.

I also felt very guilty because I never gave my father a grandchild while he was alive. I know in a way it's not my fault and that God sends us things when it is the right time, but that weighed on me. I fell pregnant six months after his passing and gave birth a couple of months after his one-year anniversary of his passing. I would often look at my daughter and wish Nonno could see her. I would tell him that I wish he were around to see her. I cried many times about the guilt I felt. Yolanda knew none of this.

First thing Yolanda said to me when I sat down was, It's ok that you weren't there." I knew right away she was referring to the morning of his passing. "Your father knows you were there with him in spirit when he passed, even if you were not beside him." I just began to cry.

Then she said, "He wants me to tell you he really likes the bumblebee. He thinks it's cute, and he wants you to know that he does see her and is around her." I started to cry even more. How could she have known about the bumblebee backpack, and that I would speak to my father about these things. My daughter did not go anywhere without her yellow bumblebee backpack, it was her favourite. He was trying to validate and prove that he was with her. That night my heart felt full. I felt at peace. Yolanda brought me peace. She provided me with reassurance and comfort and helped me to overcome my guilt as my father was able to connect with me and reassure me."

Yolanda Tarantino

-Teresa Roti-Gillette

"A good friend of mine referred me to Yolanda many years ago to help me balance my energy. Was I in for a surprise!

Yolanda was very welcoming, and she has a big heart. She also has talents beyond my comprehension. I started Reiki sessions with her and could feel the results very quickly. I couldn't wait to see her again. As time went on, we became friends and I could see that she had many more talents. Sadly, my father unexpectedly passed away and I was distraught. As we were talking on the phone, she said something which confused me. She told me that my father wished he could see my son grow up. Not my children but my son. As I already had two boys that weren't very young this left me wondering why he would have said that. A few weeks later I found out that I was pregnant and gave birth to a baby boy. I finally understood the message that Yolanda gave me from my father. I came to witness that everything she told came to fruition.

I had a court case coming up and was quite nervous. She told me it would be postponed. That morning as I was sitting in front of the judge and the only thing I could think about was that she was wrong. She was never wrong! Then all of a sudden the judge postponed the case. I couldn't believe I had doubted her."

- Rosa Macri

"When I met Yolanda for the first time, I had just lost my dad about 6 months prior. Losing my father was the hardest thing I had to go through in my life. After his death, I prayed to see him again. I prayed for him to appear in my dreams. I asked God to just show me that he was ok. That he was in a better place. I needed to know that deep inside my heart. One day in my clothing store, I was at the cashier finalizing a client's purchase. It was Yolanda and her husband. I had never seen them before. As I was writing up her invoice, she said to me, out of the blue, "By the way, your father is here with us, and he wants me to tell you he is ok, and not to worry about him."

I almost fainted. I said to her, "What did you just say to me?" She repeated what she had said and explained who she was to me. I was blown away. From that day onwards, Yolanda has been in my life. She is a trusted friend, and guidance counsellor to me and many others and whom I consider dear to me. She is spiritually connected and authentic. I am blessed she is in my life.

Not long after our first encounter, I dreamt of my dad. In my dream, I was walking into my kitchen and he was sitting on my kitchen stools, with his back towards me. There was a bright light encompassing his body and I approached closer. He whirled around to face me. He smiled the brightest and happiest of smiles as this light shone upon him. It was the happiest moment for me." -

Tonia Brindalos

Yolanda Tarantino

About the Author

Who am I?

God is always with you. We are not separate from him.

I am finally able to be my true self. However, after discovering these things about myself, I am curious to know what type of being or energy I truly am. Am I an enigma? A shaman? A medium? A psychic? Do I need to put a label on it? In the end, I realize I am all these and so much more.

I'm a human being who wants to understand who God is. I am an instrument of God's love, and I accept this beautiful gift of serving others. I've had numerous wonderful supernatural experiences, which have taught me a great deal about myself. There is immense joy when I can connect with others through readings, and when I can provide and validate the truths of their loved ones who have passed on and share their stories. Though it's easy for us to twist and contort the truth to fit our own understanding of what good and evil are, it's best to look at everything through the eyes of a child instead of sitting and judging others. We need to be present and accept the soul's presence with unconditional love.

All my suffering was a means to develop my insight and empathy. How could I relate and help others if I didn't learn to forgive my abusers? I had to be able to comfort and tell people I understood everything they were going through. I needed to be filled with compassion and empathy.

All of my supernatural experiences, all my visions, were God guiding me along the path. Even in my darkest hours, when I felt very far from God, I can always look back and see a glimpse of Him smiling and waiting patiently.

Once you let go of your pain and learn to trust in the natural process, there are no limits. Nothing is standing between you and God. Throughout my journey, the schooling, learning, and experiences, a key realization in comprehending that nearly everything that happened was necessary to bring me to this level of understanding and enlightenment.

When my soul never felt worthy of existence, I learned it wasn't someone or something that would fulfill me; it was self-acceptance and self-love that allowed me to understand what God was trying to show me—that He loves me unconditionally.

As it is said in Luke 11:34-36:

"Your eye is the lamp of your body. When your eye is healthy, your whole body is full of light, but when it's bad, your body is full of darkness. Therefore, be careful lest the light in you be darkness. If then your whole body is full of light, having no part in dark, it will be wholly bright as when a lamp with its rays gives light."

Two Paths, One Purpose:
A Journey of Marriage and Spiritual Growth

My husband, Steve, recently became ordained as a reverend. He's now the president of the Spiritual Healing Church and has been my rock. He has supported me through all the craziness in my life, including all the emotional tidal waves. I can now sit and laugh about all of it. However, some moments were not funny in the slightest, especially when I was dealing with my sexual abuse. Throughout it all, Steve was very patient and kind. He was supportive and understanding, listening to me and providing me with what I needed. What I couldn't receive from my own family, I was blessed bountifully by him. He gave me the space to heal and work out what I needed to deal with.

What makes our relationship so strong is that we recognize our individual autonomy and respect one another. We may be different, but we also have common goals. We are united and present for one another in the best and worst of times. We're on this journey of life together. I am so proud of all he has accomplished in his life, and he is also very proud of me.

It hasn't always been easy; relationships never are. We are two strong-willed individuals who occasionally clash. However, we also make each other laugh. Through Steve, I've learned to be more patient, kind, and loving. I am now able to give back.

Connecting you with your spirit is being able to see the bigger picture. I realized that perseverance was the backbone of who I am, and you need to identify and clear all the obstacles that keep you away from God so you can have a spiritual relationship with Him.

www.ingramcontent.com/pod-product-compliance
Lightning Source LLC
Chambersburg PA
CBHW071057090426
42737CB00013B/2362